from pampered
to
PRODUCTIVE

DEBBIE BOWEN

from pampered
to
PRODUCTIVE

RAISING CHILDREN WHO KNOW HOW TO WORK

Horizon Publishers
An imprint of Cedar Fort, Inc.
Springville, Utah

ISBN 13: 978-1-4621-1019-3

Published by Horizon Publishers, an imprint of Cedar Fort, Inc., 2373 W. 700 S., Springville, UT 84663
Distributed by Cedar Fort, Inc., www.cedarfort.com

LIBRARY OF CONGRESS CATALOGING-IN-PUBLICATION DATA

Bowen, Debbie, 1962- author.
  From pampered to productive : raising children who know how to work /
Debbie Bowen.
    pages cm
  ISBN 978-1-4621-1019-3
  1. Child rearing. 2. Work ethic. 3. Work--Psychological aspects. I.
Title.
  HQ769.B6583 2012
  649'.1--dc23
                        2011046452

Cover design by Angela D. Olsen
Cover design © 2012 by Lyle Mortimer
Edited and typeset by Melissa J. Caldwell

Printed in the United States of America

10 9 8 7 6 5 4 3 2 1

Printed on acid-free paper

To every parent striving to raise productive,
unpampered children

. . . .

Contents

· · · · · · · · · · · · · · · ·

ACKNOWLEDGMENTS

• • • • • • • • • • • • •

I would like to thank everyone who has had part in the success of this book:

The many friends and family who provided encouragement and expressed interest in this book while it was in the making.

Timothy Robinson, who saw the book's potential when it was far from finished. His suggestions regarding content, style, and structure improved the book dramatically.

The wonderfully helpful and accommodating team at Cedar Fort, who have spent many hours producing this book, especially my editor, Melissa.

My parents, Bob and Susie Gilham, who are some of the hardest working people I know and who instilled in me a love for and an understanding of the value of work.

My husband, Bruce, my greatest source of encouragement and support, who has spent countless hours tending the children so I could have quiet writing time and who is my friend and companion in the never-ending struggle of teaching our children to work.

And, of course, my children—Trenton, Jadee, Caleb, Camille, Isaac, Jarom, Abram, Levi, Melia, and Marissa—without whom there would have been no book to write! I am most grateful for their help and cooperation in our daily toils.

Labor is life.

Thomas Carlyle

· · · · · · · · · · · ·

Man must work.
There is no work so rude that he may not exalt it;
No work so impassive that he may not breathe a soul into it;
No work so dull that he may not enliven it.

Henry Giles

Preface
Our Family Philosophy

Love, therefore, labor;
It is wholesome to the body and good for the mind.
—William Penn

By worldly standards, we were never rich. Dad was a school teacher and Mom was a homemaker. Consequently, we didn't have much money, we didn't go on many vacations, and we didn't own expensive play toys. Yet somehow we never felt disadvantaged. We were rich in other ways. My mother, the daughter of German immigrants, and my father, of Native American descent, who spent his teenage years on the reservation, knew firsthand the value of perseverance and self-reliance in making something of themselves; and they passed on to their five children a legacy of thrift and industry. There was meaning and substance to our lives that could not be purchased with money.

We grew up in a small farming community with acres of alfalfa, corn, and sugar beets. "Home" was a quiet neighborhood at the end of a dead-end street surrounded by an empty field, a small farm with a barn and pastures for horses, and neighbors with large lots on which they grew impressive gardens. It was a happy childhood full of many pleasant memories—making houses in the nearby field by trampling down the alfalfa to form rooms; late night yard games with the neighborhood children; fresh vegetables from the garden; homemade bread; playing in the irrigation water; racing with my sisters to see who could shell the most peas; and early morning raspberry picking "parties," as my sisters and I sarcastically called them. Our family was typical of many of the neighbors, except that on our two-thirds of an acre we raised a variety of animals—chickens, ducks, geese, and even a baby lamb—and we grew not one but two large gardens that produced an abundant supply of vegetables to weed, harvest, and preserve.

My mother, who grew up on a dairy farm in upstate New York, understood the value of hard work, and we children became the unwilling beneficiaries of her unceasing ambition. We preserved everything Mom could get her hands on—peaches, pears, cherries, apricots, apples, berries, corn, peas, beans, beets, tomatoes, and spinach. I have vivid recollections of long summer days shelling bucket after bucket of peas and snapping the ends off of piles and piles of beans. When the beans in our garden ran out, Mom picked the neighbors' surplus. Sometimes I wondered if she did it just to torture us! Although the days were long and hot and the work was often tedious and messy and performed begrudgingly, the experience of working side by side with my siblings has created cherished memories and built friendships that continue to this day.

My husband too lived on a small farm in a rural community during his early childhood and has fond memories of helping to care for rabbits, chickens, pigs, a horse, and a cow. He also helped irrigate, weed the garden, and pick fruit. Although he was still quite young while living on the farm, his yearning for that lifestyle never left him.

As a result of our upbringings, my husband and I felt a strong desire to continue these agricultural traditions with our own children. Our first home was on one-third of an acre, nearly half of which was in garden. We also had fruit trees, raspberries, dairy goats, chickens, turkeys, and a dog. The children helped plant, water, weed, harvest, and preserve the vegetables in our garden; and we bought a variety of fruits and berries which were either canned or dried or made into juice, jam, jelly, or syrup. In addition to canning, the children were expected to help with the yard work—planting flowers, weeding, trimming, edging, and mowing. At age eight, they were taught to milk the goats and were included in the rotation for milking, gathering eggs, and feeding and watering the animals. When the outside chores were finished, they helped with a variety of tasks inside as well—cooking, cleaning, ironing, dusting, washing dishes, and babysitting.

In today's world of pampered children, indulgences, allowances, and self-gratification, it almost sounds like child abuse. However, we later moved from that little house on one-third acre, and it was interesting to listen to the children reminisce fondly about what they missed most—the garden, fresh corn-on-the-cob, home-canned peaches, baby chicks, and especially the goats. In fact, one son insisted that he would have goats when he grew up.

And, in fact, he did. At age eighteen, he spent his own money to purchase two female Boer goats. A few months later, one had twins and the other had triplets. Thus began a wonderful chapter in our family's book of adventures. We have spent many happy moments watching the miracle of birth unfold in our backyard barn. Our children have learned about service and sacrifice while bottle-feeding baby goats whose mothers had abandoned them and caring for fragile newborns in cardboard boxes in the kitchen. And they have learned about the cycle of life when some of those newborns did not survive.

As hard as the work is and as much as they may complain at the time, something happens between the weeding and the watering, the milking and the mowing, and the cooking and the cleaning. More than a garden is grown, more than animals are tended, and more than meals are made. In the midst of working, they have learned to love those they serve and with whom they serve, even the animals. Lifelong friendships are formed, memories made, and emotional bridges built that connect parents to children and sibling to sibling.

Of course, farming is not the only way to teach children to work. Opportunities for work are as varied as the individual. A brick mason can teach children the skills of his trade; so can a plumber, an electrician, a jeweler, a grocer, a seamstress, a chef, a woodcarver, or a fisherman. It is not so much about the type of work children do as it is about having a work experience. Working with and for others provides an enduring connectedness that will span the years.

Today's modern conveniences that are theoretically meant to improve the quality of our lives may not be all they initially appear. Food processors, dishwashers, and snow blowers may have eliminated the need for many people to be working at once, but they have also eliminated the opportunity to work together—learning to understand and get along with others. While we would not want to return entirely to the lifestyle of our grandparents, we would do well to analyze the necessity of our modern conveniences, recognizing what we are giving up for the advantages we may gain.

Our family does not use a dishwasher. When the children complain, we simply say, "Why do we need another one? We have eight already!" Unfortunately, they fail to see the humor in this as well as failing to see the advantages of standing side by side at the kitchen sink—telling stories, singing songs, reciting scenes from a movie, and, yes, even arguing. Although they may not realize it now, their relationships with one another are being strengthened. Hopefully, in some future day they will recall these dishwashing days fondly.

Working together has been a way of life since families began. In agrarian societies, a family's very existence is dependent upon the efforts of all its members. At very young ages, children assume adult responsibilities—chopping wood, clearing fields, hauling water, milking cows, feeding chickens, digging ditches, fixing meals, tending babies, and sewing clothes. No one questions the necessity of the work—children or parents. It is their way of life. And contrary to the popular sentiment of our day, it doesn't hurt them. What it does do, however, is turn them into responsible adults with grit and character who understand the value of work and self-reliance.

In time, difficulties and challenges make men out of boys. It makes adults out of children. It creates depth of character and gives substance and meaning to our lives. Many of society's most respected leaders have come from difficult circumstances. They have known hardship and poverty and overcome incredible odds, but have you ever heard them complain about their early morning paper routes, hauling hay, milking cows, or performing menial labor in order to make a few dollars to support their widowed mothers? On the contrary! These are the very things they tout as the stepping-stones to the heights of greatness they have achieved.

Years ago I was with a group of women who were discussing this very topic. An older woman in the group mentioned that when her children were small they did their chores without being asked. They just knew what was expected and did it. There were a few "oohs" and "ahhs," and I even heard someone remark, "Well, they don't do that today."

What an unfortunate commentary on our society. What has happened to our parenting in recent years? Have we become too soft? Do we give in too easily? Do we make too many excuses for our children? Are they involved in too many things? Are we turning out selfish, lazy, ungrateful children who think the world owes them a living? Perhaps, in the spirit of good parenting, we think our children need to be pampered and protected. But I believe today's children—yours and mine—can still be taught to value work. It's all a matter of establishing realistic expectations, providing adequate training, and holding them accountable for the stewardships we assign them.

Whether you live on thirty acres or the thirtieth floor of a high-rise apartment building, opportunities can be found to teach your children to work. The size of your lot and your home are irrelevant when it comes to teaching children to do a job well and to see it through to completion. Capability, dependability, and responsibility are some of the greatest gifts we can give our children. They will forever bless the lives of your children. They are skills that are greatly lacking in the work force today.

Hard work, especially family work—the very work we do in our homes on a daily basis—can do much to change our children, our families and, in fact, our entire nation.

> Home is the center from which we define and understand the nature of everything we encounter in the world. The home . . . is not one thing among many in a world of things; nor is it merely the product of a culture. Rather, the world of things derives its sense, and a culture its significance, from their relationship to the home. Without the home, everything else in the world or in a culture is meaningless. . . . By changing how we do family work, we can build character, link families, unite communities, and change nations. . . .
>
> Helping one another nurture children, care for the land, prepare food, and clean homes can bind lives together. This is the power of the home economy, and it is the power, available in every home no matter how troubled, that can end the turmoil of the family and begin to change the world.[1]

We must not underestimate the healing power of working with and serving one another. It is therapy for the soul. As someone keenly observed, "The heart is the happiest when it beats for others."[2]

Notes

1. "World Congress of Families II," Kathleen Slaugh Bahr, Geneva, Nov. 14–17, 1999, http://www.worldcongress.org/gen99/speakers/gen99bahr .htm.
2. "Modern Proverbs," Protestant Apologetics and Theology, http://www .ovrlnd.com/MainPage/modernproverbs.html.

I

CHANGING YOUR MIND-SET

*Opportunity is missed by most of us because it is
dQ dressed in coveralls and looks like work.*
—*Thomas Edison*

***B**renda's day begins early*. At 5:00 a.m. she sets out break-
fast and throws in a load of laundry. Then she prepares for
work intermittently while braiding hair, dressing children, signing
papers, and counting lunch money. Sighing heavily, she drops the
children off at school on her way to her paid job. After work, she
does more laundry, shuttles children to soccer practice and piano
lessons, listens to her first-grader read, practices spelling words
with her third-grader, prepares dinner, irons a shirt, sweeps the
floor, vacuums the living room, and makes a batch of cookies for
the PTA bake sale. Near midnight she falls into bed exhausted.
Overworked and overwhelmed, she feels resentful of her husband
and children.

Sharon is a stay-at-home mom with three preschoolers. Every
day is the same endless chain of chores. With a cranky baby on
her hip, she runs here and there in a frenzied state—wiping noses,
changing diapers, washing dishes, folding laundry, cooking and
cleaning, vacuuming and dusting. But, at the end of the day, nothing

seems to look any better than it did in the beginning. All she has to show for her work is tousled hair, a toddler-smudged sweatshirt, and makeup long since vanished (if she had any on in the first place). There are cracker crumbs in the carpet, dirty dishes on the counter, dirty laundry already piling up *by* the hamper, and footprints across the freshly-mopped kitchen floor. Discouraged and disheartened, she wonders, *Why bother?*

Tom and Tonya left their children alone for a few hours while running errands. Upon their return, they found that a home-made hurricane had just hit their place, leaving a trail of damage in its wake. The kitchen was cluttered with dirty dishes and bits of food from their children's unrestrained, relentless prowling for sustenance. Toys were strewn about the house in chaotic fashion while the little ones ran dirty, half naked, and unattended. No homework had been done, and the older children were lying about the house engrossed in television and computer games, oblivious to the damage and destruction going on around them.

Sound familiar? If so, this book is for you!

HOUSEWORK MAKES YOU UGLY

Years ago, my mother-in-law gave me a little wooden, starry-eyed doll with kinky hair that pokes out in all directions. The caption on front reads, "Housework makes you ugly." For a long time it sat on my kitchen counter—a cruel reminder of the reality of my situation.

My husband didn't like it. He thought it sent the wrong message to the children. I must confess, I secretly delighted in it. It validated my feelings of anger and frustration, and I found silent sympathy in it when I felt tired and grumpy.

It's not that I mind housework so much—I just find it aggravating and annoying to clean the same thing five times in one day. I get tired of being a human street sweeper, running around tidying up after the children. And, even worse, I get tired of them coming along right behind me destroying everything I have just tidied up!

Discussing this dilemma with a group of mothers long ago, one mother lamented, "At the end of some days, I feel like a great big spit-ball." What a vivid description of some of our less-memorable mothering days! I have reflected on her words many times over the years.

I once read a newspaper article describing the incredible pressures women today feel regarding housework. The article suggested hiring a housekeeper. While this is certainly one solution, for many mothers it is cost-prohibitive. Furthermore, it deprives our children of valuable opportunities for work and service. Part of the solution to our housecleaning woes lies in better training of our children, thereby allowing more time for organizing and managing the household, catching up on unfinished projects, or perhaps even pursuing some long-neglected personal interests.

The driving force behind the writing of this book has been *you* and the many mothers like you that I have met over the years. The look of exasperation in their eyes and the sound of resignation in their voices over getting their children to help around the house have motivated me to share my experiences. Hopefully, you will discover a more beautiful you as your work is accomplished more efficiently and you are left feeling less tired, less grumpy, and, consequently, less ugly.

POOR MANAGEMENT SYNDROME

Before going any further, let's take a quick survey[1] to determine whether you suffer from Poor Management Syndrome. Answer *yes* or *no* to each statement:

- I have a good idea of what I want to accomplish, but I don't seem to be getting anywhere.
- I always seem to be giving orders of one kind or another.
- I'm always checking on my children to make sure they carry out assigned tasks properly.
- I do a lot of housework at night when the children go to bed.
- When I'm gone for any length of time, the house is a disaster.

- My children are slow or reluctant to make decisions on their own.
- I get so bogged down with household chores that I don't have time for me.
- I suffer fatigue, high blood pressure, or chest pains.
- My children are frequently bored or watch too much television.
- My children usually complain when asked to help with chores.
- I believe if you want something done right, you've got to do it yourself.
- By the end of the day, I'm too exhausted to go anywhere or do anything with my spouse or family.

Did you find yourself saying, "Yes, yes, yes"? If so, this book is definitely for you.

I WAS RELUCTANT TO DELEGATE IN THE BEGINNING

Shortly after the birth of my fourth child, I learned the value of getting children to help around the house. As a homeschool mom with a new baby, and a two-year-old, four-year-old, and six-year-old, I was overwhelmed. Additionally, my husband was working full-time while finishing up a dissertation for his doctoral degree in the evenings. To say that life was busy was an understatement.

One evening after a tearful account of the day's events, my husband felt compelled to offer some advice. (All I really needed was a listening ear and a little sympathy.) After a quick computation of all available data, he came up with the simplest, most logical answer and said frankly, as only a man can say, "You need to get the children helping more."

"Oh, sure!" I protested. "What can a two-, four-, and six-year-old do?"

He then proceeded to suggest several tasks—mopping floors,

cleaning the bathroom, vacuuming, folding laundry, emptying the garbage.

I winced. "Not my babies! They're too little for such manual labor. *I'm* the mother; it's *my* job to take care of them. Besides, they wouldn't do a very good job anyway; and it would be more hassle than it was worth."

But my husband persisted. We had a lengthy discussion—my husband suggesting tasks that I felt were above my children's abilities, me countering with excuses about why they couldn't or shouldn't do them. I must admit, I was rather skeptical; but then I really didn't have a choice. I could either continue doing what I was doing, which was obviously not working, or I could try his way. At length we reached a compromise on the tasks the children would be assigned, and I reluctantly agreed to give it a try. (I figured a few weeks would be sufficient time to prove it wouldn't work, and then we would go on with life the way we always had.)

A few days later, we held a family council. Little did our children know that their simple, carefree lives were about to change forever. First, my husband enumerated all the responsibilities we had as parents and how hard it was to do it all. Then, he made the proposal that the children would assume some of these tasks to lessen the burden somewhat.

After listening intently, six-year-old Trenton asked inquisitively, "How long do we have to do this?"

"Forever," my husband replied too quickly.

There was considerable silence while Trenton mulled this over and then timidly declared, "I would be glad to help . . . but not forever." We had to do some serious backpedaling to make it not seem as though they had just sold their souls, and at last they agreed to help.

The family council was essentially for the two oldest children, and this is the list of chores that were delegated to them at that time. Although they had already been doing many of these tasks on a sporadic, informal basis, they now became *permanently delegated* tasks:

mopping kitchen and bathroom
folding underwear/matching socks
setting and clearing the table
emptying the garbage
cleaning the bathroom
folding cloth diapers (It was
long ago!)

dusting
cleaning up toys
helping with canning
vacuuming
making their beds
preparing simple meals

I know it seems like quite a bit for a four- and six-year-old, but I was amazed at how well they did. I was also amazed at the difference it made for me. There *was* a way; there *was* hope; these little children could make a difference. As much as I hate to admit it, my husband was right.

Since that first family council, our family has grown considerably and so have the children's responsibilities. We eventually bought a small home with a large lot on which we planted a good-sized garden. Naturally, the list of delegated tasks increased. Today, we live on three and a half acres with one-half acre in lawn, an even larger garden, grapes, berries, fruit trees, a variety of animals, and several beehives; and, again, the children's responsibilities have grown as well. Today their chores include:

weeding/watering garden and
  flower beds
picking vegetables
ending beans/shelling peas
drying fruit
dressing and bathing younger
  children
washing dishes
gathering eggs
feeding/watering the animals
shoveling snow

raking leaves
mowing the lawn
preparing meals
changing sheets on beds
ironing
helping with laundry
irrigating the pasture
changing oil in vehicles
sweeping patio and porch
shoveling manure
mending fences

At first glance, it seems like a lot. But before you are tempted to turn us in for child abuse, remember, they don't do all these things every day nor do they do all of these things year round. And, again, I am impressed with how well they have done and at the difference it makes for me.

CHILDREN ARE ASSETS, NOT LIABILITIES

Effective delegation occurs when we begin to think of our children as assets rather than liabilities. Perhaps, like me, you sometimes find yourself starting a countdown for bedtime right after dinner (or perhaps before). Or maybe you can't wait for the children to start back to school at the end of a long summer vacation. Instead of viewing the time our children are home as a hectic, miserable experience merely to be endured, we can make use of this valuable time by having projects for them to do. Not only will the time pass more quickly for everyone, but it will also be much more pleasant. By tapping into our children's vast reserves of time and energy, we can fill their spare time with worthwhile activities while simultaneously teaching them the value of work *and* completing many of our own overdue projects.

Summer and other school breaks are great opportunities to get some concentrated help from your children. Instead of bracing yourself to barely survive this time off, plan projects that will bless your life and theirs. During the summer, we grow a large garden and do a lot of canning, enjoying the fruits of our labors all winter long. On shorter breaks, we sometimes clean closets or dresser drawers or work on projects that require more than a Saturday to complete. And a relaxing way for me to unwind after Christmas is to tie a quilt while watching movies and enjoying quiet time with my family.

One summer my children and I all worked together refinishing three wooden chairs that had been in our shed for years. My husband had threatened to throw them out several times, but I kept insisting that I was going to use them. I decided this would be the summer—before it was too late.

Every morning, right after chores were completed and before everyone started their individual projects, we sanded on the chairs for thirty to forty-five minutes. It took six of us two months of serious sanding to complete the project, and for a while it looked as though we had taken on an impossible task. I must confess, if I had been doing it alone, I probably would have given up, but since the children had already invested so much time, I felt obliged to finish. Nevertheless, when the chairs were at last stained and varnished, complete with new cloth seat coverings, we all felt the satisfaction that comes from knowing we had accomplished something difficult yet wonderful. It was a powerful bonding experience for all of us. Fourteen years and several new cloth coverings later, those chairs are still part of our kitchen.

YOU ARE THE CONDUCTOR OF YOUR OWN HOME ORCHESTRA

For a moment, imagine yourself as the conductor of a great orchestra. It is opening night. As the curtain parts, the audience is stunned to see a solitary figure standing on stage. After playing a few notes on the violin, you run to play the trumpet, then the tuba, then dash back to play the violin again. Not only would it take an incredibly long time to get through a piece of music, but the resulting sound would be choppy and disjointed and, in fact, most unpleasant. And, I am guessing no one would stick around to hear the end of it! Certainly, no one would argue the merits of individual musicians playing a single instrument that, when blended simultaneously with an entire orchestra, produced a symphony of beauty and harmony.

As strikingly absurd as this example is, we are often oblivious to similar situations in our personal lives. Housework is not a one-man (or woman) show. As the parent, you are not a soloist but rather the conductor of your own home orchestra. You need not—in fact, you *should not*—try to do all the work yourself. There is no need to run haphazardly from task to task trying to make melody out of discord and chaos. Like musicians in an orchestra, each member of the family should have specific, individual assignments—thus establishing a symphony of siblings. Your job is to compose a family masterpiece by orchestrating the delegation of various assignments to ensure that the work is completed in an efficient, timely fashion, everyone working together harmoniously (at least once in a while).

To set the stage, let me begin with an example of what can happen with effective delegation. One Saturday, I had gone to an early morning meeting, leaving the house around 7:00 a.m. When I returned two and a half hours later, my husband and seven children had already dressed, eaten breakfast, washed the dishes, cleaned the kitchen, made their beds, scrubbed the bathrooms, vacuumed the floors, and my eleven-year-old son was just finishing with the mopping in the kitchen. The house felt calm and quiet and clean, and I sank into a comfortable chair for a brief respite to unwind from a busy morning.

Before you jump to any conclusions, let me assure you it is not like this every Saturday. In truth, some Saturday mornings we are just finishing breakfast at 9:30 and still trying to get started on the day. This particular morning my husband was exceptionally ambitious, and I was pleasantly surprised *and* most grateful.

The point of this story is to help you realize that you don't have to do it all. Children can work without you there, and the house doesn't need to fall apart just because you are gone. "No one can whistle a symphony."[2]

FATHERS ARE INVALUABLE

While much of what is said in this book is focused at mothers, who typically bear the greater burden of running the household, it applies equally to fathers. Their support and cooperation is crucial. Mother and father should provide a united front in the formidable task of raising children who know how to work.

The more Father is involved, the more effective delegation becomes. I appreciate it when my husband assumes the responsibility for getting the children working. It temporarily relieves me of the burden and is a welcome break. Besides, it's no fun being the only bad guy in the family. Delegation works best when there are no disagreements between parents on what will be done, how it will be done, or who will do it.

Fathers tend to be better delegators. Whenever my husband oversees a task—inside or out—I can generally be sure he will get several of the children helping. Delegation seems to come more naturally to men. (I am still trying to decide if it is a deliberate attempt to diminish the delinquency of their children or a sheer act of desperation.) Either way, you would do well to capitalize on this innate character trait.

My husband enjoys doing Dutch oven cooking. It is his hobby, so to speak. What this really means is that he prepares the pots while the children are busy in the kitchen—chopping, stirring, dicing, cutting, and grating. My husband spends most of the time giving orders, tapping the briquettes to keep them burning, and poking the food with toothpicks to see if it is done. It has become a family joke that whenever Dad decides to do Dutch oven, most, if not all, of the family will be involved in some way. We enjoy giving him a hard time about it, and he takes it good-naturedly. Whenever he tells someone that he does Dutch oven cooking, the rest of us just smile, casting sideways glances at each other. After all, we know the truth!

But then, that's exactly what delegation is all about—accomplishing great things through others. And *we* don't really mind because in the end we all benefit from a delicious dinner. I have to admit, he does come up with some good ones—barbecued ribs, lemon chicken, cheesy potatoes, and the best berry pie you have ever tasted! He always says, "Everything tastes better when it's cooked in a Dutch oven."

Fathers can be great role models. The mere presence of Father alters the mood in the home, and children often work better when he is around, especially if he sets the example. This is particularly important for boys. In addition to the traditional male tasks, let your sons see Dad cooking, sweeping, vacuuming, bathing children, and changing diapers. Father can have a profound influence on his children's attitude toward work, and this most important responsibility should be shared between both parents.

MANY HANDS MAKE LIGHT WORK

Levi, Melia, and Marissa were helping me in the kitchen—preparing dinner for that day *and* making a casserole and dessert for the following day. We worked busily for more than an hour, making significant progress. At length, Marissa, recognizing the value of our combined efforts, said to me, "This would take forever by yourself."

"Working together works."[3] That's what delegation is all about—working toward common goals, everyone sharing the work and doing their part. It's about teaching children to take pride in what they do and being accountable for the tasks that are theirs, thereby experiencing the subsequent feeling of success and self-respect that comes from achievement. Together you can accomplish great things.

I AM NOT AN EXPERT

Before going any further, I need to give a brief disclaimer: I do not have a degree in child psychology, home management, or delegation, nor have I had any professional training on the subject. My only training has been "on-the-job" in the ongoing struggle to raise ten children. In no way do I profess to be an expert, *unless* an expert can be defined as someone who has learned something through a lot of trial and error and a lot of tears and frustration. Under this definition, I most definitely qualify!

Most of what I have learned and what I will share has come from the school of hard knocks *and* from a deeply held personal conviction of the power of work and the merits of a good day's labor. Over the years I have refined and added to this process of delegation, and I have learned a few tips that I will share with you. I hope you find them informative and useful.

Notes

1. Harold L. Taylor, *Delegate* (New York: Warner Books, 1989), 25–28. (The wording was changed slightly to fit a home situation.)
2. H. E. Luccock, http://quotes4-u.blogspot.com/2010/08/no-one-can-whistle-symphony.html.
3. Dr. Rob Gilbert, "HeartQuotes: Quotes of the Heart," http://www.heartquotes.net/teamwork-quotes.html.

2

DELEGATION—
YOUR KEY TO SANITY

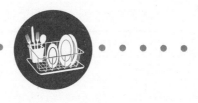

*The only place where success
comes before work is a dictionary.*
—*Vidal Sassoon*

WHAT IS DELEGATION?

Camouflaged Slave Labor

My husband facetiously defines delegation as camouflaged slave labor, and I must admit, sometimes our children think that's exactly what it is. When my daughter, Jadee, overheard me give this definition to a friend one day, she exclaimed indignantly, "Mom, there's nothing camouflaged about it!"

However, a more scholarly definition can be found in Harold Taylor's book, *Delegate: The Key to Successful Management:*

> Leadership is not the process of accomplishing great things by ourselves. . . . It is rather the process of accomplishing great things through our [children], thereby raising their self-respect. Leadership also involves more than simply overseeing or directing others. It

involves developing [children's] skills through delegation. . . . [Delegation]. . . does not mean dumping work onto someone without prior training . . . or constantly delegating to the same [child]. Nor does it mean always assigning all the boring, meaningless tasks. . . . Delegation develops people who are able to work independently with a minimum of direction.[1]

"If your actions inspire others to dream more, learn more, do more, and become more, you are a leader."[2] "Leaders don't create followers, they create more leaders."[3] Family counselor James Dobson puts it quite succinctly, "Our objective as parents . . . is to do nothing for boys and girls which they can profit from doing themselves."[4] And Paul Lewis has said, "Remember, your basic job as a parent is to work yourself out of a job."[5]

The true test of successful delegation is how well your children work alone or when you are gone. One of my most liberating days was the Halloween when I left to go on a bike ride forty-five minutes before we were to go trick or treating, leaving the children— ages nine to seventeen—with instructions to be in costume when I returned. That was the best Halloween ever!

Permanent Delegation

Basically, there are two types of delegation—permanent and spontaneous. *Permanent delegation*, as the name suggests, refers to assigned tasks that children know they need to perform daily, weekly, monthly, or seasonally. Thursday night may be their night to do dishes, or they may need to feed the dog every morning before going to school, or perhaps it is their job to shovel the driveway each time it snows. They know it is expected of them and they can plan for it.

When my two little ones first started folding underwear and matching socks, it was a monumental task, sometimes taking two hours to complete because they dawdled so much. Each week when I did laundry, they knew they would be expected to match socks, and so it was with great anxiety that they would ask, "Is today sock day?"

My children also know they will be expected to clean up their toys when they are finished playing. One day, five-year-old Jarom wanted to play with the Daktari jungle set. This ends up making quite a mess with trees and cages and jungle animals scattered across the living room floor. Nevertheless, as I carried the box to the living room, he informed me that he would clean it up because "that was just part of life."

At our home, we have a rotating daily schedule for washing dishes, rinsing dishes, and sweeping the floor. Our more thorough housecleaning is done on Saturday, and we have a rotating schedule for these chores too. The children know they will be held accountable for the completion of their work—and sometimes, on their own initiative, they will do their chores Friday afternoon if they have commitments Saturday morning.

The specifics of what will be done and who will do it were decided in a family council where everyone had a chance to give input. The secret to successful permanent delegation is accountability and appropriate consequences when assigned tasks are not completed (see *Discipline*, p. 32).

Spontaneous Delegation

The second type of delegation is *spontaneous delegation*. This means tasks or assignments that are delegated due to extenuating circumstances such as illness and emergencies. At this time, for example, I call the children together and explain that Dad has invited someone to dinner and I need help preparing food and tidying up the house. Each child is then assigned one or more tasks; and somehow we manage to clean the house, set the table, and prepare the food with a delicious aroma filling the air as my husband, all smiles, saunters in the house ten minutes before the guests arrive!

I remember one spontaneous incident vividly. It was Trenton's fifteenth birthday. Just as I walked into the kitchen to begin preparing his special birthday dinner, his younger brother entered from the opposite direction, carefully cradling his right arm with a look of pain and panic. One look at the unusually large lump protruding from his wrist told me that it was broken. My mind immediately began spinning. What to do with the broken arm? (This was a new experience for us.) Should I call my husband? Should I call the doctor? And what about the birthday dinner? Should we postpone it until another night? After making a few phone calls, I gathered the children together, explaining that Dad and I would be taking Caleb to the hospital. I then proceeded to give instructions to each of the children. One would be in charge of cooking the noodles, another the sauce, another the salad, and someone else would set the table. After everything had been assigned, we left the house.

When we returned two hours later, I was surprised by what I found. Not only was dinner ready, but the table was also set, complete with tablecloth and candles; the drapes were drawn; and soft, classical music was playing, providing a pleasant retreat from our hectic afternoon. I guess Trenton figured if he had to make his own birthday dinner, he might as well make the best of it!

Mother Bunny Delegates

We have a classic children's book *The Country Bunny and the Little Gold Shoes,* which illustrates perfectly what can happen with successful delegation. It is the story of a little girl bunny whose secret desire is to one day become the Easter Bunny. As time passes, however, she ends up getting married and having twenty-one baby bunnies. With all those babies to care for, it seems that her dream of being the Easter Bunny will never come true.

But as the babies grow older, Mother Bunny realizes that her little bunnies are now capable of assuming more responsibilities around the house, so she calls them all together to give them assignments. She teaches some of them to sweep, some to mend and sew, some to make beds, and some to cook, wash dishes, do laundry, and work in the garden. With her children now doing much of the work, Mother Bunny once again has spare time.

Eventually, the Easter Bunny dies, and Mother Bunny decides

to audition for his job. The problem is that wise, old Grandfather Bunny doesn't think a mother with twenty-one babies could possibly take on this important assignment. Mother Bunny then carefully explains how each of her children has individual tasks, allowing her time for other things, and Grandfather Bunny at last agrees to let her be the new Easter Bunny.

On Easter Eve, after Mother Bunny has been out all night delivering goodies, she returns home to find "that the garden was tended. . . . The floors were swept and there were two lovely new pictures painted and hanging on the wall. The dishes were washed and shone in the cupboard. The clothes were washed and mended and nicely hung away. And her twenty-one children were all sound asleep in their little beds."[6]

I know exactly what you're thinking: *Cute story, but it's just a fairy tale. It never happens that way in* real *life.* But what if I told you it *could* happen that way. In fact, I can tell you from personal experience that it *has* happened that way in our home—more than once, by the way, which leads me to believe it wasn't an accident. It is wonderful to know that things are taken care of while we are gone, and my husband and I often express our appreciation to the children for their diligence.

RULES OF DELEGATION

Amazing things can happen with delegation. I am still amazed at times, even after all these years. However, there are a few simple rules for success. I will refer to these rules throughout the book, so it is important to understand them now. They are

- Be Firm, Be Fair, Be Flexible
- Be Patient
- Be Tolerant
- Be Specific

Rule 1: Be Firm, Be Fair, Be Flexible

In other words, be consistent yet considerate. Make rules, set guidelines, and establish appropriate consequences for disobedience. At the same time, recognize that children have extenuating circumstances too. Be willing to adjust.

Be firm. Don't give in to your children's fussing or complaining just because they're trying to get out of work, they're angry about doing the work, or they're eager to play or watch television. They need to understand that they have responsibilities around the house, and they will be expected to complete them. (See *Discipline,* p. 32.) If, for example, your child whines about feeding the dog, remind him that part of the agreement for getting a dog was that he would care for it. If he delayed until it was cold and dark outside, the dog still needs to be fed.

Be fair. Be sensitive to the needs and abilities of your children. Set reasonable expectations. What is fair for one child, may not be fair for another. Tailor tasks to fit their unique capacities and circumstances. Thus, you can challenge them without overwhelming them.

While my fifteen-year-old is quite capable of vacuuming the entire house, I would not expect the same of my five-year-old, although she could certainly vacuum a room or two. Likewise, I might ask my eighteen-year-old to pick all the apples on the apple tree, but this same task would overwhelm my eight-year-old. A more realistic assignment for him would be to pick a bushel or two a day—a task he could accomplish because it had limited parameters.

At our home, the children join the rotation of dishwashing, housecleaning, and lawn mowing when they turn eight. However, one son was rather small for his age, and at eight, he was definitely too small to mow the lawn. Therefore, we waited a year before assigning him this task. Even at nine, he struggled to mow his section of the lawn, and we often helped him with the chore.

Be flexible—allow for their emergencies. If a child has an important test or school project due the next day and it's their night to do dishes, let them trade with another child. If a child is too sick to do their work, move on to the next person in the rotation or have everyone pitch in and cover for them. If someone has an activity that requires them to be gone all evening, don't holler to them as they walk out the door, "The dishes will be here when you get back!" No one likes to come home at ten o'clock at night to a messy kitchen and a sink full of dirty dishes.

One summer, my daughter took a microbiology class at the local university. Due to the intensity of the class, we didn't ask her to do much yard work. Besides, the other children were out of school and had more free time, and it wasn't too burdensome on them to pick up the slack.

Be careful that your children don't take advantage of your kindness. There can be a temptation for children to be "sick" longer than necessary, to always have a lot of homework, or to drag one project out in order to avoid helping with a second project. Everyone has an occasional emergency, but, as the word implies, emergencies occur infrequently. Be careful that they don't become a habit.

As you are sympathetic and compassionate to your children in their moment of crisis, they will reciprocate. One evening as I planned the following day's events, I had a mild panic attack. I needed to do laundry, can apricots, pack for a family camping trip, and go shopping. In order to give myself a head start on the day, I washed the canning jars and sorted the apricots the night before. Still, it was a pretty daunting proposition, and I went to bed feeling rather discouraged.

The next morning I approached the kitchen dismally, dreading the burden of the task before me. But what I found caught me completely by surprise. There on the counter were twenty-five quart jars filled with apricots, ready for canning. I was stunned! Apparently, Trenton, Caleb, and Isaac had secretly set their alarms for 5:00 a.m. and quietly washed, pitted, and bottled the fruit while I slumbered. It was one of the nicest things anyone has ever done.

Rule 2: Be Patient

It will probably take your children longer than you expect to get the hang of it, especially your little ones. Little children are still mastering their hand-eye coordination, and those little hands—and even the not-so-little hands—can be slow and awkward at times. (Except, of course, when they're getting into things they shouldn't.) Seemingly simple projects can be major events for children.

If you ask your eight-year-old to cut tomatoes, for example, you need to allow sufficient time for completion of the project. First, he will need to methodically sort through all the knives, carefully selecting the one most suited for the project. Perhaps he will even need to try several of them to determine which one works best. While washing tomatoes, he will probably be distracted by the running water, becoming enthralled as it cascades over the dirty utensils he has found lying in the sink. Or, as the sink fills with water, he may become so absorbed with the various floating objects that he completely forgets about the task at hand. Sometime later, you will find him happily splashing about—not a care in the world!

Children are immune to many of the pressures we feel as adults. Time meant nothing to my four-year-old son. I was talking to him about an upcoming event one day, explaining that it would happen "tomorrow." Curiously, he asked, "What's tomorrow?" This little guy measured time and days by events: Sunday was church day, Tuesday was laundry day, and Saturday was when Dad and all the children were home. At our house we have granola for breakfast on Sunday because it is quick and easy when preparing for church. On occasion when we had it on a day other than Sunday, this same little guy would look at me and innocently ask, "Is today church day?"

Deadlines, time constraints, and multi-tasking are foreign concepts to small children. Speed is simply not an issue. Be patient, as frustrating as it may be at times—in fact, much of the time. Delegation is a process, sometimes a long, slow process depending on the age and capacity of your children. If you can remember that the goal is not speed but raising responsible, capable children, patience will come much easier. Teaching children to work is an investment in their future, and while some dividends may be slow in coming, they will definitely be worth it.

Rule 3: Be Tolerant

Be willing to accept less than perfection. Closely linked to patience is the third rule of delegation—tolerance. Again, keep in mind that the goal is raising responsible children.

I remember well my own internal struggle when four-year-old Jadee first started mopping the bathroom floor. It was not as clean as I would have liked, and I agonized over my conflicting feelings. One side of me understood how important it was for her to do this job by herself, yet the other side of me wanted the job done well. At length, I opted to forego my own need for cleanliness, accepting her best effort for the sake of the greater good that would be achieved in the long term. With practice, her work gradually improved.

Occasionally, however, when I just couldn't live with it, I locked the bathroom door and redid parts of the floor, being careful that she never knew. If children find out you've redone their work, the negative results are two-fold: first, their self-esteem suffers—they didn't do a good enough job; and, second, they learn that they really don't have to do a good job because Mom or Dad will just do it again anyway.

The quality of the work is not nearly as important as the lessons your children are learning. This is especially true with young children. While helping me in the yard one day, three-year-old Melia stated solemnly, "I'm a good helper." I'm not sure how much she really helped, but at this tender age her perceptions of herself mattered most. The rest would come later. Naturally, the older the child becomes, the greater your expectation that the work be done well.

At any given moment, there is bound to be clutter somewhere. Before I was married, I had visions of an immaculately clean home—tidy drawers and closets, spotless countertops, neatly made beds, and bathroom chrome that sparkled. Today, with ten children, I have learned to tolerate a certain degree of clutter. Unless I spend all day cleaning house, it simply isn't possible—or reasonable—to keep it completely clean all the time.

I once heard someone say that their home was clean enough to be healthy but dirty enough to be happy. That is a truth worth remembering. While there is great disparity in clutter tolerance, don't be unrealistic or too demanding.

Someday, when the children are grown, I will wash down all the walls and straighten all the drawers and closets. When I wander from room to room, there will be a place for everything and everything will be in its place. Imagine! How peaceful. How serene. How eerie . . . and quiet . . . and lonely. But that day is not today. Today I am raising kids, and kids create clutter.

Rule 4: Be Specific

Never assume anything. Too often we take it for granted that our children will know how to do simple projects, only to find out later, much to our chagrin, that they really didn't. Being very specific at the outset about what you want done and how to do it can prevent a lot of frustration for parent and child.

When asked if he would clean the bathtub, one young man wondered whether he should clean the outside too. A bit surprised by the question, his mother answered, "Why, yes." When she came to check on him later, she found him spraying off the outside of the tub with the shower massage!

Isaac tapes the bag of laundry soap. One day, I opened a twenty-pound bag of powdered laundry soap to refill the bucket I keep in the laundry room. I used about one-third of the bag and asked Isaac to "roll down the top of the bag, tape it up, and take it back downstairs." He seemed happy to help and went off without any questions. I didn't think any more about it until a few days later when I went to the fruit room to get something. There was the bag of soap, well secured with about ten long strips of duct tape—up each side and across the top! *Ugggh*, I thought. *What has he done? That is* *too much tape!* This thought was immediately followed with, *He did exactly what you told him to do.*

When I asked my son to "tape the bag," I had a mental picture of what I expected—one little piece of masking tape in the center of the bag, just enough to keep it rolled down; but I had failed to convey any of this to him. He really wasn't trying to be difficult. His vision of "taping" was just different than mine. A few simple instructions could have ensured that we both shared the same vision.

HOW DO I BEGIN?

The Six D's of Delegation

Now that you understand the basic rules of delegation, you are ready to tackle the big question that has probably been nagging at the back of your mind all along, "*How* do I start?" The process of teaching children to work is outlined in what I call the *Six D's of Delegation*. By following these basic steps, you can tailor a system of delegation unique to the needs of your particular family:

- **Decide:** choose which jobs will be delegated
- **Divide:** assign jobs to each family member
- **Deliberate:** hold regular family councils
- **Demonstrate:** provide adequate training
- **Discipline:** administer appropriate consequences
- **Determination:** hang in there!

The First "D": Decide—Choose Which Jobs Will Be Delegated

Deciding which jobs will be delegated is the first step of delegation and, perhaps, one of the more difficult. This is the time for personal introspection as you ask yourself some hard questions:

- Why is delegation even important or necessary?

- What do I hope to accomplish?
- What are my personal and emotional needs?
- What jobs am I willing to delegate to my children?
- How much are they capable of doing?

There will be a real temptation to make excuses for your children or to feel guilty about passing on some of "your" work to your children. It is only natural. We all want to be the nice guy, but this is the time to be serious and sensible about what *you* can do and what *your children* can do. When it comes right down to it, it really isn't "your" work anyway. It's the family's work. Your children dirty the bathroom; there isn't any reason they shouldn't help clean it. They wear the clothes in the hamper; there isn't any reason they shouldn't help wash them. And they eat dinner, so there isn't any reason they shouldn't help prepare it and clean up afterwards.

For your own sake and for the sake of your children, resist the urge to be too lenient. Remember, delegation is not just about the benefits *you* receive by passing on some of the work. More important, it is about creating work for your children, thereby keeping them busy and out of mischief, raising their self-esteem, and teaching them to be responsible. A pampered child is not a productive child.

After you have done some serious soul searching, discuss your plan with your spouse. Maybe he can help you brainstorm. He may even make suggestions you haven't considered. Even if he doesn't have much to add, it is critical that he is aware of the plan *before* you present it to the children and that the two of you are in complete agreement—or have at least reached an acceptable compromise. You don't want him to come unglued when he discovers that your ten-year-old washed the family car or that your teenager is on the roof cleaning out rain gutters!

When the two of you have ironed out all the wrinkles, you are then ready to present your plan to the children. This should be done in an official family council, thereby creating the impression that it is something important and that you are serious about what you will be discussing. (See *Deliberate,* p. 27.)

The Second "D": Divide—Assign Jobs to Each Family Member

I have already mentioned how the division of chores was done initially in our family when the children were still very small. It was a decision my husband and I made, afterward informing the children of their new duties. This worked fine when they were young, but I can guarantee this approach will not work well with older children—especially teenagers.

Everyone should have a voice in the division of chores. With older children, we now sit together and discuss various options as a family, eventually reaching an agreement on what will be done. Sometimes we reach this conclusion by general consensus; other times we vote on it. It is important to note that while we try to please everyone, everyone may not be completely happy every time. Compromise is an important part of family life.

You may not get it right the first time. After a few weeks, you may realize that one of the chores takes longer than the rest or that one child is not quite capable of completing his assignment. Gather the family together to make refinements and redistribute tasks.

When our three younger boys first started emptying the garbage, it was always a fight. First, they complained because they didn't want to do it; and when they did do it, they fought over which garbage cans they would empty and who had emptied more than another. I got tired of the hassle.

Finally, I decided to try a different approach. I assigned each of the boys specific garbage cans for which they were responsible. It worked great! There was no more fighting over who had done more than another or who should do what. It was a small change, but it made a big difference.

Years ago, when the older children first started doing dishes, everyone helped clear the table, then two of the children washed and rinsed the dishes. Clearing the table took forever. For some reason, it seemed to be an agonizing chore. My guess is that the washer and rinser weren't excited about clearing the table *and* doing the dishes, so they tried to clear as little as possible. Because they were working so slowly, everyone else did too. Everyone was subtly trying to do as little as possible.

For a long time, I wondered what could be done to make things go more quickly. Finally, I decided that if the washer didn't clear the table, they could get started immediately on the dishes. This helped somewhat, but then we had the problem of dishes piling up in the rinser's sink because they were still busy clearing the table. It became obvious that the rinser should also be excused from clearing in order to help with the dishes. Things got a little better with this approach, but we still had trouble getting the table cleared. The dishwasher often finished washing everything on the counters and had to wait for the table to be cleared.

At last I came up with what has turned out to be—if I do say so myself—a clever solution. If the table is not cleared by the time the dishwasher gets everything washed on the counters, the clearers must wash the remaining dishes. It has worked marvelously!

There have been a few times the washer "got them," as we call it. But the greater problem, if you can call it a problem, was that the clearers were too efficient. Sometimes they started cleaning up before I even finished my meal. Between cutting meat, buttering toast, checking food in the oven, and caring for the baby, it took me longer to eat than the rest of the family, and there were times when my plate was swiped away from me with food still on it!

The division of chores is constantly changing. Almost as often as the seasons change, the way we do chores changes as well—school lets out or starts again, someone gets a new job and isn't home in the evening to do dishes, someone is old enough to join the rotation, someone moves out, or someone moves back in. This is where you really get to practice flexibility. It is also where family councils, as discussed in the next section, become so important.

During the summer we have a dishwashing rotation that changes each meal—one child washes, one rinses, and one sweeps the kitchen floor. When school starts again, however, the dishwashing schedule also changes since all of the older children are gone during the day.

The children who are home have a separate lunch rotation. We have also had to do some pretty tricky maneuvering with our college-age children to accommodate their busy schedules. At one point, it got so complicated that we had to keep a list to remind us who had to wash dishes on which days.

Delegation is constantly changing and evolving. Just when you think you've got a system that works, something is bound to change. Accept it, work it out, and move on. Remember, flexibility is the first rule of delegation.

The Third "D": Deliberate—Hold Regular Family Councils

Family councils are similar to board meetings. They are the coming together of questions, complaints, and concerns. This is the time to work out disagreements and find solutions to your problems in an environment of cooperation. That is not to say that some of these "discussions" don't get rather loud and lively, but everyone must be allowed to express their point of view without fear of ridicule from family members. They must feel their contribution is important and that their vote counts. There will be some give and take by everyone, but you should eventually be able to reach a compromise that is satisfactory to all.

If my husband or I feel strongly about a certain issue or about how something should be done, we will move the conversation in that direction. And sometimes we may detect hurt or anger in one or more of the children and will work to alleviate those feelings. We have also found that we may need to help them come to closure as there is a tendency to rehash the same things over and over. As long as the debate isn't out of control, however, we let them work out many of the details of what and how things will be done themselves. After all, they are the direct beneficiaries of the discussion.

A family council in action. When we moved back from Hawaii, we needed to decide how the chores would be divided in our new home. So we sat together as a family, discussing possible ways to divide the chores. There was considerable discussion, and many possibilities were presented before we finally arrived at a satisfactory solution. This is what we came up with:

- Person 1—mopping kitchen and entryway, dusting, mowing part of lawn
- Person 2—vacuuming entire house, mowing lawn
- Person 3—cleaning master bath, mowing lawn
- Person 4—cleaning laundry room and bath, sweeping back porch, mowing lawn
- Person 5—cleaning main bath, sweeping front porch, mowing lawn
- Jarom, Abram, Levi—emptying garbage cans

A few months later, we cut out the carpet under the kitchen table, replacing it with linoleum since carpet under the kitchen table wasn't working with small children. This greatly increased the amount of kitchen mopping to be done, so we met as a family and discussed what to do. It was decided that the entryway would now be mopped by the person who cleaned and mopped the laundry room.

When our son Jarom turned eight, we had another family council. We have found that eight is a good age to move children out of the smaller jobs and blend with the older children in the dishwashing and housecleaning rotations. Now that Jarom had reached this magical age, we needed to discuss what he would do and how the chores would be redistributed to include him.

After much debate, it was finally decided to keep things simple for him at this time. He would take on the task of mopping the entryway and sweeping the back patio every week in addition to his regular job of emptying garbage. However, since he was doing more work on Saturday, his two younger brothers would empty his garbage on that day. We also decided that Abram, now almost seven, could take on the added responsibility of sweeping the front porch.

Gradually increase responsibilities. We have found it easier to get children working if their responsibilities increase gradually.

Abram had been making his bed and emptying garbage for years. He also helped set and clear the table, clean up toys, and pull weeds. He was now assuming the added responsibility of sweeping the front porch and helping with lunch dishes. When he turned eight, we would add even more. This way we could ease him into the work cycle without overwhelming him.

Weekly planning meetings are another dimension to family councils. With three teenagers and a twelve-year-old who thought she was a teenager, we found that we needed to have a weekly planning meeting to discuss their various activities. On Sunday evening, we gather with the calendar to write down the events of the week. Not only does this help with scheduling, but it also helps see potential conflicts with chores and how they can be resolved. Someone may need to switch nights for doing dishes or, due to some family activity, Saturday chores may need to be done on a day other than Saturday. If the children know this ahead of time, there will less complaining and fussing later in the week when you remind them of the change.

That's the beauty of family councils—to analyze what is and is not working and to come up with satisfactory solutions. In the end, everyone is clear about what the new plan is and how it works. And, hopefully, everyone is happy with it. Do not underestimate the ability and willingness of your children to help work through problems. They can come up with some rather insightful solutions. After all, they have a vested interest in the final decision.

The Fourth "D": Demonstrate— Provide Adequate Training

Adequate training is essential to successful delegation. Without it, you end up with a lot of sloppy work and a lot of frustration. This takes time—sometimes a lot of time if your children are still small— but the investment is certainly worth it. A few hours of careful training now will reap large dividends in the days ahead.

There are three important areas to cover when training your

children on new tasks: what, why, and how. Don't just tell your children *what* to do and *how* to do it, you must also tell them *why* they need to do what they're doing. Go through the entire process, step by step, discussing and asking questions as you go. By asking questions rather than merely showing or telling them what to do, you encourage critical thinking *and* active listening, which leads to long-term retention. In other words, next time they do the task, there is a better chance they will remember how to do it!

At our house, we mop floors with a bucket of water and a rag so we can better clean the edges and the corners. Several years ago when my daughter started mopping the kitchen floor, I noticed it was taking much too long to dry—sometimes more than an hour— and it was frustrating when I couldn't get into the kitchen to do my work. After a couple of weeks, I finally told her to wring the rag out better so the floor wasn't so wet. Then I began to notice that the floor didn't seem to be getting as clean as it should, so I decided to watch her mop. First, she squeezed the rag so completely dry there was hardly any water left, then with it still wadded in a little ball, she proceeded to mop. The problem became obvious immediately. Not only was the rag too dry to really clean, but with it all rolled up, she was missing parts of the floor as she swiped it back and forth. Clearly, the dirty floor was a reflection of poor training; and right then we had a lesson on mopping the floor.

Dipping the rag in the bucket, I pulled it out dripping wet. "What's wrong with this?" I asked. (Notice the use of a question that helps the child think through the process.) Then I wrung the rag so tightly that there was no water left in it. "What is wrong now?" I asked, and we discussed the problem of squeezing too much water out. Next, I showed her the correct way to wring the cloth and showed her how to mop so that the entire floor was cleaned. These few minutes invested in proper training solved the mopping problem.

Likewise, when we plant the little seeds in our garden in early spring, each of the children is responsible for watering two or three rows every day until the seeds sprout. We have shown them the correct procedure for watering—a small stream of water gently trickling over the newly-planted seeds as the hose is moved slowly back and forth over the rows. If the children had only been shown *what* to do without explaining *why*, they may assume that by turning the water on twice as much, they could get done twice as fast and unintentionally wash away all those tiny seeds. Or they may hold the hose too long in one place, causing erosion. And, yet, despite our deliberate demonstrations, we still had to plant the carrots three times one year!

Irrigating the pasture. Speaking of gardens, we have a never-to-be-forgotten story illustrating the need for specific explanations when delegating duties. By way of explanation, Utah is carved into miles of irrigation ditches, enabling water stored in mountain reservoirs to water crops and fields of this desert landscape during the hot summer months. A system of weirs and head gates channels water to the correct location, each person opening their own head gate at the beginning of their irrigation turn and closing it at the end to allow the water to flow on to the next field.

On this particular day, my husband helped my son get started irrigating early in the morning, then left for work, telling him to be sure to close the head gate when our turn was over. At the appointed time, however, my son noticed that our ditch was beginning to empty and assumed that the next person had taken the water, so he felt no need to close our gate. We didn't know we had a problem until later in the day. When Camille went out to water our newly-planted garden, she noticed a steady stream of water was flowing from the ditch. Since we had never had that much water in the garden, I immediately quizzed my son about closing the head gate.

He explained that he had not closed it because the water in the ditch looked like it was going down. Only now did he see the error of his decision, and he promptly ran to close it. Even with the gate closed, however, water continued to flood into the garden for two more hours as the ditch emptied. Our efforts to divert the water were futile, and we ended up with a garden almost completely covered with several inches of standing water.

It was nearly two days before the water finally soaked into the ground and at least another week before the ground dried out completely. We worried about the tender tomato and pepper plants and whether the seeds in the ground had been washed away or would even sprout. All we could do was wait.

To make matters worse, Utah was experiencing a three-year drought, and water was at a premium. In our little community, we were surrounded by farmers whose livelihood depended on every precious drop of water, and we felt guilty about our seeming extravagance. Located alongside the road, our garden was easily visible to passersby, and for several days I lived in dread of being reported for a water-conservation violation.

Luckily, this story has a happy ending. We were never accused of any crimes, and, miraculously, the new little plants survived and even the seeds sprouted. The potatoes, however, came in poorly; we ended up replanting some of them. Much to our surprise, we had a very productive garden that year. And my husband learned an important lesson about discussing with your children *why* they do *what* they do.

Washing an onion. Another example of the need for clear directions occurred as I was revising this very section years ago. The baby started crying, so I walked into the kitchen to get her just as my eight-year-old son was preparing to peel an onion for a Dutch oven meal my husband was "fixing," which means that several of the children were also in the kitchen—scrubbing, peeling, stirring . . . but we've already discussed all that.

Anyway, my son was at the kitchen sink washing an onion he had pulled from the garden. My husband walked to the sink just in time to see him dip the onion in the warm, soapy dish water. "Don't wash it like that!" he scolded. "You don't wash onions in soapy water." And then in a more apologetic tone, he added, "But I guess I didn't clarify that when I asked you to *wash* the onion."

"This is perfect," I shrieked. I was just revising the section on never assuming anything and always discussing the *what, why,* and *how* when assigning tasks. Embarrassed, my son hung his head. I tried to encourage him by saying, "Don't feel bad. This will make a great story for my book!"

I think you get the point. It's such a simple thing, but it's easy to assume that some things don't need explaining. Children need more. They do not have the benefit of age and experience. What may be clearly obvious to you, may not be at all obvious to them. Many mistakes can be avoided with a few minutes of explanation.

The Fifth "D": Discipline—Administer Appropriate Consequences

How often, while pondering your children's carefree attitude toward work, have you thought, *Something has got to change around here?* Determined to improve behavior, you implement a course of action. Perhaps you even go to the extra effort of making a job chart to inspire productivity. There is immediate improvement, but two weeks later you're back where you started. Chances are, it all falls apart due to a lack of discipline.

Discipline is the most important aspect of delegation—it will make or break the whole process. Without discipline, delegation is merely a lofty goal. Ideally, children should work out of duty, love for parents, or a sense of belonging in the family; but, as you well know, we do not live in an ideal world. Therefore, children must be taught responsibility. Discipline has three aspects:

- Accountability
- Consequences
- Consistency

Accountability

Accountability is an absolute. When delegating, there is a tendency to focus on the process of making assignments and providing adequate training, often overlooking the most important step—accountability. Accountability means that a child is personally responsible for their assigned tasks, and when they fail to complete them, there will be consequences. It is a pretty simple concept, but it can be difficult to enforce. It takes time—lots of time, *and* effort—lots of effort. It can be mentally, emotionally, and physically draining, but it is, nevertheless, vital to successful delegation.

Many frustrated parents bemoan the fact that their children will not cooperate. Some have had family councils, some have taken the time to train their children, and some have even gone to the trouble of making elaborate job charts. But, all too soon, the enthusiasm wears off, and they find that nothing is getting done. The parent is left wondering, *Where did I go wrong?* The answer is accountability.

That which is reported on, gets done. There needs to be a follow-up plan. Children need to know that someone will be checking their work, not only to see that it is done well but that it is done in a timely fashion. They must know that if either is found lacking, there will be consequences. In simplest terms, accountability means that you hold your children responsible for their responsibilities.

Consequences

Every behavior has a consequence. This statement is prominently displayed on our refrigerator. It is a gentle reminder to the children that they are free to choose their behavior, but they are not free from the consequences of their choices. Years ago we had a family council to define this really big word that tends to have a negative connotation. We explained that there are negative and positive consequences. If they do their work well, the positive consequence is that they are free to do other things. If they don't, there will be a negative consequence.

At our home, when the little ones are disobedient, we usually sit them on a chair for a time out. Before they can get off the chair, we give them a "talk." During this talk, we discuss what they did or did not do and what they could or should have done instead and how they can improve in the future. We also point out that in the time they have been sitting on a chair, they could have had the assigned task completed. Instead, they have spent their time sitting on a chair, and now they still have to do their job. We end with a few words of encouragement and a hug.

For the older children, the consequences are greater. We have found that assigning an extra task to the one already assigned is very effective—washing walls, washing windows, cleaning a cluttered drawer, or straightening a closet. This kills two birds with one stone—the child gets disciplined *and* I get some of those neglected projects completed.

Some mothers have wondered whether using work as punishment won't cause children to dislike work. We have not found this to be the case in our home. What is does help children realize is that it is much better to do the *first* job in a timely manner to avoid having a second job. Furthermore, the way *you* handle discipline makes a difference in *their* attitude.

Be sure the consequence fits the crime and the criminal. In other words, "Never use a cannon when a water pistol will do."[7] Being too lenient engenders indifference while being too harsh begets resentment and rebellion. I have learned a clever strategy for getting this right the first time. If, for example, I find my child goofing off when he should be doing the dishes, I will say something like, "You have five minutes to start on the dishes or there's going to be trouble." Or, if I pass by the bedroom and notice my son playing Legos and his bed unmade, I will say, "If I come back in fifteen minutes and your bed isn't made, there is going to be a consequence." The child is then left to wonder, *What kind of consequence? What kind of trouble?* Perhaps he may even imagine something far worse than I had in mind, which will be enough to get him moving.

More important, this vague, ambiguous threat gives me time to cool off a bit while contemplating an appropriate consequence—one that hasn't been hastily uttered in the heat of the moment. (Screaming and hollering and ranting and raving are not consequences.) I can't tell you how many times I have gone to my room to rock back and forth in my chair while contemplating an appropriate consequence for a disobedient child. Sometimes I am so angry, I want to lash out with something really harsh—like washing every window in the house—a punishment I will probably regret later. As I rock and ponder . . . rock and ponder, allowing sufficient time to cool down, I am able to think more rationally and eventually come up with something appropriate.

This technique has spared myself and my children many rash, unrealistic threats such as, "You're not going to the party tonight!" or "You're grounded for a week!" I once heard a mother say, "You're grounded for a month!" Very few situations warrant that kind of punishment and even fewer parents will follow through. Remember, when you punish a child, you punish yourself too. Make sure it is something *you* can live with. Once the discipline has been issued, stay firm. Don't back down or turn soft. And don't give in to whining and pleading and promises to never do it again.

One day my ten-year-old son had been especially disobedient. As a last resort, I gave him an ultimatum—start cooperating or he wouldn't be able to play with friends that afternoon. He didn't heed my warning, and I finally told him he couldn't play. A few hours later, he had two phone calls from two different friends inviting him to play. Time had passed, things had settled down, and my feelings of frustration were gone. Even though I knew the initial punishment was justified, I desperately wanted to give in, but I also knew that by relenting, my future attempts at discipline would be greatly diminished. This was definitely one of those times when the punishment hurt me more than it did him. Even the most well-deserved discipline can be difficult to enforce, especially on a long-term basis—hence, the need for carefully considered, reasonable consequences. (That may require a lot of rocking!)

Discipline need not be long-term in order to be successful. For this very reason, I am not a big proponent of grounding. I feel it is used too frequently and too often inappropriately. It seems to be the cure-all for many of the problems we encounter with our children. Generally, grounding is not very effective because it is difficult to enforce with the passage of time and the cooling of tempers. Furthermore, a young child has a hard time making the connection between not making his bed in the morning and not being able to ride his bike that afternoon. Something firm and prompt is much better—the child sits on a chair, then makes his bed, and moves on with life. Or an older child does his "extra job" in addition to the job he should have done, and the discipline is complete.

The more closely connected the correction is to their noncompliance, the more effective it becomes. For example, our ten-year-old daughter was having trouble getting her bed made before school in the morning. Repeated pleadings and adequate warnings produced no results. One evening my husband came home from work, and her bed was still unmade; so he pulled off all her bedding and told her to remake the entire bed. He then told her that the next time the bed was not made, the same thing would happen. That single incident made such a profound impression that we have never had a problem since.

My children's orthodontist related a similar incident from his youth. At the high school one morning while all the teenagers were mingling in the halls, he heard his name over the intercom followed by this request, "Please come to the office so your mother can take you home to make your bed." I would be willing to bet he never went to school with his bed unmade again!

Another time, I was having trouble with my daughter putting her clothes in the hamper inside out. This went on for several weeks—becoming worse with each succeeding week. Repeated requests for help in this matter got me nowhere, and one day after spending an extra twenty minutes turning all of her dirty clothes right side out, I gave an ultimatum—anything left inside out would be set aside for her to wash by hand. Apparently, she didn't think I was serious because the next week there were several articles of clothing which I set aside for her to wash that evening. Interestingly enough, that solved the problem.

My sister-in-law had a problem with her son's clothes not even finding their way to the hamper. Every week, it was a miserable game of hide and seek—hunting for clothes in the closet, under the bed, and scattered across the floor. Tired of the ongoing battle, she picked up all his dirty laundry one day and hung them on the tree in the front yard—underwear and all. There they hung when he disembarked from the school bus in front of all his peers! Somehow the clothes managed to make it to the hamper after that.

Negative and Positive Motivation. The consequences mentioned above are forms of negative motivation—a child does something wrong and something unpleasant happens. Of course, positive motivation—a thank you, a hug, a compliment, a reward—is the better choice. However, when a child is especially rebellious or consistently disobedient and all else fails, as it surely will from time to time despite our best efforts, stronger action must be taken. (See *My Children Refuse to Work*, p. 73).

Help your children understand that consequences are a direct result of choices* they *have made. This can be done simply, directly, calmly, and lovingly by saying something like, "I'm sorry you didn't mow the lawn last night. I guess you *chose* to wash a window today." You can even add a bit of humor, "I see you didn't do the dishes. That's so nice of you to *volunteer* to wash a wall. I've got one that's really dirty."

If they protest, remind them of the family council where you discussed and agreed upon acceptable consequences. Be sure to stress the fact that *they* made the decision not to obey, and by so doing, *they* made the decision to accept the consequences that accompany that disobedience. This puts the responsibility back on them—where it belongs.

Don't feel guilty; you're not the bad guy. I am reminded of a scene in the movie *Dennis the Menace* where Mr. Wilson is ranting and raving about what a terrible son Mr. Mitchell has and that Dennis is no longer welcome to visit. As Mr. Mitchell drives away, Mr. Wilson hollers after him, "I'm not the bad guy in this, Mitchell. I'm the victim!" So it is with your children. Don't let them make *you* out to be the bad guy when they are disciplined for *their* disobedience.

This is especially important for mothers to remember. We tend to be more softhearted and sympathetic. Too often we give in rather than see our children "suffer." I know. I have a problem with this myself. I tend to nag and nag, giving them several chances rather than face the problem straight on. What usually happens is that I get all worked up. The volume of my voice escalates along with my blood pressure, creating more stress and tension for myself than necessary. The repeated nagging only teaches my children that they don't need to mind the first time, creating a habit of disobedience.

My husband is much better, and I have learned much from watching him. When he asks a child to do something and discovers later that it hasn't been done, he issues the discipline coolly, almost in a whisper. There is no anger, no stress, no escalating tension. I marvel at how easy he makes it look.

Consequence is the inseparable companion of choice. It is important for children to learn that as they sow, so shall they reap. They need to understand the law of consequences; life is full of them. Failure to allow them to experience the natural consequences of their behavior only prolongs the inevitable, making the eventual discovery that much more difficult. They need to understand that to a large degree _they_ are responsible for their own happiness or misery depending on _their_ obedience or disobedience.

Consistency

Consistency is crucial. To be effective, consequences must be applied consistently. It doesn't take long for children to learn whether or not you mean what you say. When they realize you are serious, they are more apt to obey. However, if they know that you regularly go back on your word or that you rarely follow through, they are more willing to take risks about being obedient, hoping they get lucky. Repeated threats without action become hollow and meaningless.

A few years ago, I was having a problem with my younger boys doing what I asked them to do—simple things like making their beds and emptying the garbage. I kept getting after them—nagging, scolding, threatening—but they didn't cooperate. At last it dawned on me that I was not being consistent in issuing consequences.

Something has got to change, I decided. *I need to be more firm. They need to know that I mean business.* So I settled on a course of action and began the new program.

The next day I asked four-year-old Abram to make his bed. When I came back a while later and discovered that he had not done it, I said, "Abram, look at me." (I learned from a friend years ago that making eye contact increases the probability that they are listening.) Looking him in the eye, I said firmly, "I want you to make your bed. If I come back and you're not doing it, there is going to be a consequence."

He immediately threw himself on a chair, whining in a distressed, frantic voice, "Mom, you have to give me a billion chances!"

"No, you don't get a billion chances," I replied. "You get one."

I was tightening up, and he didn't like it. It took a while for my boys to get used to our new way of doing things, but they eventually caught on that I was serious, and things got much better.

Consistency between parents is also important. It is important that both parents make the effort to follow through with discipline. Children are quick to pick up on any disparities between parents. They know which parent is more lenient and will play one against the other, if you let them. Therefore, it is important to be in agreement about what chores will be done, who will do them, and the consequences for not getting them done. Do not contradict each other in front of the children. Any disagreements should be discussed in private, approaching the children only after the two of you have reached a mutually acceptable consensus.

Some days can really be draining, especially with young children. Some days it may seem that they spend more time on a chair than not and that you spend most of your time disciplining. It does get better. Trust me. If you can hang in there through their learning curve, it will eventually register in their little developing minds that it is much better to obey. In time, there will be less nagging, less scolding, less threatening, and more cooperation. It really is a much better way.

The Sixth "D": Determination—Hang in There!

Hang in there—*you can do it!* I will be the first to admit that delegation is not easy. It is not a big-bang effort and then you're done. It is a daily, ongoing battle. It requires a lot of effort today, and tomorrow you will wake up and start all over again. Some days I wonder why I even try. One day the children are excellent, cooperative workers. The next day they are silly and ornery, and it's a struggle all day to get them moving. And, as you know, it really isn't fun trying to get children to do things they really don't want to do. Sometimes I feel like I'm pushing water up hill with a rake. You will experience failures, but keep trying! As they say, success is getting up each time you fall.

Go ahead and cry . . . or take a long walk, a hot bath, or hide out in your room for a while—whatever it is you do to relieve stress. If you think it's bad trying to get one or two or three or four children to work, try ten! Some days it is just too much. I feel like Alexander in the popular children's book who is having a "terrible, horrible, no good, very bad day."[8] I am a volcano ready to explode. When I get too overwhelmed, a fast bike ride in the fresh country air or a few minutes weeding in the yard can be very therapeutic. Sometimes, though, I fling myself on the bed and let it all out in a good cry. All the stress, all the frustration, all the anger seems to come out through my tears. In fifteen or twenty minutes, I'm ready to face the children again.

"Tears cleanse your mind and soul of stresses, strains, and frustrations. . . . [They] are as potent as laughter when it comes to physical and psychological relief. Crying provides an emotional release that can lower blood pressure and reduce emotional and muscle tension."[9]

One day was particularly bad. It was laundry day, and there had been more loads than usual. When my daughter got home from school, I asked her to hang a load of clothes outside on the clothesline. She told me "no," muttering something about why did *she* have to do it and why wasn't anyone else working. I ignored her comments, hoping she would give in without a confrontation.

An hour later she still had not done it, and it was now time to leave for piano lessons. I asked her in a firm, don't-you-dare-say-no voice if she would please hang the clothes before we had to leave—in ten minutes. While she hung the clothes, I finished up a few loose ends, all the while uptight about leaving since we also needed to pick up my son on the way.

When my daughter didn't come in right away, I decided to grab the clothes out of the dryer and take them to my room so they would be ready to fold when I returned. Upon opening the dryer, I discovered it was empty. My first thought was that my daughter may have already taken them to my room. But my second, more incredulous thought was that perhaps she was at that very moment outside hanging the dry clothes on the line. (Inconceivable!) A quick check of the washing machine with the wet clothes still inside confirmed my suspicion.

Now fuming, I hollered outside for her to take the clothes off the line and bring them back inside. When she came in, I ranted something about hanging dry clothes on the line, all the while throwing wet clothes into the basket. I then told her to hurry and hang the wet clothes because we were now late for piano lessons.

I finished up a few more little projects while waiting for her to come in. Fifteen minutes later, she was still hanging clothes and seemed to be deliberately making it take longer than necessary, so I decided to leave without her. By now I was so angry, I could spit fire.

It was a good thing I had a twenty-minute trip because it took me that long to cool down. All the way, I was thinking of appropriate consequences. It had to be something significant enough to make up for her difficulty with chores *and* for missing piano lessons. I decided she would work for the next two hours—washing walls and helping with dinner.

When I got home, I had cooled off enough to discuss the problem in a civil tone. We talked about her disobedience when I had initially asked her to hang clothes, pointing out that the problem wouldn't have been nearly as bad had she done it an hour earlier when there would have still been time to fix it without being late.

My younger boys didn't make the day any better. Before I left for piano, I told my younger boys to clean up their toys and be prepared to help when I returned. Just as I walked in the back door, I saw two of them walking across the back lawn toward the swing. I called for them to come inside, and then went about my work. Apparently, they hadn't heard me—or pretended not to. When I realized they had not come in, I called them again, asking them to cut up a melon. Then I went to my room to put the baby to sleep. They cut up the melon and immediately ran back outside to play. I returned to find them gone again and the melon—that was to be for dinner—mostly eaten!

I hollered out the back door for them to get the clothes off the line. When they came in, I planned to ask for more help. However, they outsmarted me by sending four-year-old Levi in with the clothes, who dropped them off at the top of the stairs and ran back outside.

I was *not* happy. Calling them in—again—I asked them to set the table, which they quickly did. And a*gain* they were off, scattering throughout the house in several directions—anywhere to avoid getting caught by Mom to do more work.

Once more, I got them all together and explained sternly that I needed their help and that I expected them to stay where they would be available to help. It was like trying to catch baby chicks. As soon as I caught one, the rest ran away. *Why does it have to be so hard?* I lamented. *Why can't they just stick around and be helpful?*

When I had time to think about it later, I realized it was mostly my fault. I kept asking them to do one thing, which they obediently did and then scampered off, assuming they were finished. Had I brought them together initially, explaining everything that needed to be done, they would have known exactly what was expected, and I wouldn't have had nearly as much trouble. Determination was the only thing that kept me going that day—determination to teach my children in spite of their lack of interest in learning and determination to endure despite the challenges.

Humor can be a great stress reliever. I know it's nearly impossible at times, but try to see the humor in the hubbub that surrounds you. Step back from the situation. Call a friend. Write in your journal. (Someday you will be able to laugh about it.) At the end of some days, I entertain my husband with the day's events. Somehow when I'm rehearsing to him the chaos and confusion of the day, it can actually be funny—even hilarious.

Other times it isn't so funny. Sometimes I complain bitterly how so and so did this and so and so wouldn't do that and how there was grumbling and complaining and fighting and sloppy work. He listens politely. Then, with a wry smile and a quizzical look, he will ask sarcastically, "Didn't you write a book about this?"

Nodding my head dismally, I respond (sometimes through tears), "Yes . . . yes, I did . . . but it's a lot easier said than done."

Theory and reality can be miles apart. Sometimes I fail miserably. The basic philosophy is not hard, but the daily grind can be a challenge. I have had enough successes, though, to know that theory and reality occasionally do converge. It is for those times that I continue to persist. I am determined to stick with it in spite of the challenges and difficulties—for my children's sake and for the good that I believe will eventually come of it.

Notes

1. Taylor, *Delegate*, 15–16, 22, modified.
2. John Quincy Adams, "Former Posse Leader: Leadership Requires Vision, Belief, and Influence," *Huntsman Alumni Magazine* (Salt Lake City, UT: Hudson Printing Company, 2011), 5.
3. Scott Marsden, quoting Tom Peters in "Former Posse Leader: Leadership Requires Vision, Belief, and Influence," 5.
4. James Dobson, "The Objective of Parents," http://parentingunited.sg/2011/02/the-objective-for-parents.
5. Paul Lewis, http://www.zona-pellucida.com/perspect2.html.
6. DuBose Heyward, *The Country Bunny and the Little Gold Shoes,* (New York: Houghton Mifflin Company, 1967).
7. Patricia H. Sprinkle, *Children Who Do Too Little* (Grand Rapids, MI: Zondervan Publishing House, 1996), 126.
8. Judith Viorst, *Alexander and the Terrible, Horrible, No Good, Very Bad Day* (NY: Aladdin Books, 1987).
9. Hope Health Letter, July 2004, vol. 24, no. 7.

3

ELIMINATING STUMBLING BLOCKS TO YOUR SUCCESS

In idleness there is perpetual despair.
—*Thomas Carlyle*

Most parents, I believe, understand the value of work and really do want their children to do more around the house. It is certainly not a lack of desire that keeps us from teaching our children to work. Most often, it is a lack of knowledge about how and where to start, which we have just addressed. Furthermore, on any given day, we may encounter stumbling blocks that prevent us from being as effective as possible in our efforts to delegate.

We try to do too much. We feel sorry for our children. I know I did when I first started, and I still struggle with that today. Sometimes without even realizing it, we make excuses for our children and ourselves that get in the way of helping our children become what we really want them to become. And, sometimes our children resist our efforts to teach them. Perhaps you have encountered some of these stumbling blocks:[1]

Misplaced Focus:

I can do it faster myself.

If you want it done right, do it yourself.

I find it enjoyable.

I'm a creature of habit.

I'm not organized enough.

I feel sorry for them.

They don't do it my way.

I'm starting too late in their lives.

My children aren't capable.

Resistance from your children:

My children are too busy.

My children complain.

My children refuse to work.

Some children work better than others.

My teenagers are intolerable.

My children expect to get paid.

Delegation is hard enough without any unnecessary obstacles. In the sections that follow, I will address each stumbling block, discussing the underlying principles and possible remedies. I hope you find solutions that will assist you in your efforts at successful delegation.

I CAN DO IT FASTER MYSELF

Principle—The greatest investment you can give your child is your time.

Of course you can do it faster yourself. How many times have you done it? You have had many years to refine and hone your skills. Think back to the first time *you* tried to clean the bathtub, mop the floor, or make a batch of cookies. How long did it take?

I can still remember the first time I made lasagna as a teenager.

It took all day. I did each step separately and consecutively. It didn't occur to me that I could cook the noodles *while* I fried the hamburger. That one meal was a major event, and I can still remember wondering how my mother did it all.

Even as a new bride it took longer to do my work than it does today. I've learned a few tricks over the years. I've learned to work faster and smarter. In fact, I have learned or, rather, been forced to learn to do several things at once.

When you first begin to delegate, you may not notice immediate results. In fact, initially, delegation may create more stress and take more of your time, especially with young children. The first time you assign a task, you will need to show the children *what* to do and *how* to do it while discussing *why* they do it. The next few times, depending on the job that needs to be done and the age and capacity of the children, you may need to show them again or at least be available to answer questions and check their work. Soon enough, however, they will be able to perform the task easily and without assistance. That is when the payoff *finally* comes. In the meantime, remember *patience, patience, patience.*

Stay nearby. In order to avoid a lot of frustration during this training phase, make yourself accessible by working near the child, occupying yourself with simple projects that don't require a lot of concentration. If I am engrossed in deep cleaning the basement, I will become agitated with continual interruptions, especially if I have to keep traipsing upstairs. However, by planning work that can be easily interrupted, I can lend assistance without becoming grumpy, thereby making it a more pleasant experience for everyone involved.

In spite of their inexperience, two or three children working together can actually complete a task much faster than you could by yourself. Remember, many hands make light work. Take the laundry, for example. It would take me quite some time to match a week's worth of socks for a family of twelve, but when everyone helps, the pile disappears in minutes.

With my first seven children I used cloth diapers. It took approximately twenty minutes to fold five dozen diapers myself. However, when several of the children worked together, it went much faster. In fact, they liked to have races to see how quickly they could finish. The record was one minute, forty-five seconds! There is no way I could have ever done it that quickly myself.

Let me emphasize again—be patient. Speed is not everything. Think of your home as a mini ATC—Adult Training Center. The goal upon graduation is to turn out productive, unpampered adults who perform well in a variety of areas. So what if it takes eighteen years to master some skills? A little investment of your time now will reap immeasurable rewards in the years to come.

IF YOU WANT IT DONE RIGHT, DO IT YOURSELF

Principle—You get what you expect.

If you expect little, you'll get little. Most children know just what they can get away with and will perform at that level. You set the standard.

Basically, there are three reasons a child is not performing at your desired expectations—capacity, poor training, or lack of accountability. In this section we will discuss the first two reasons; accountability has already been discussed. (See *Discipline,* p. 32.)

"Nothing comes from nothing. Nothing ever will."[2] In other words, you've got to let your child practice if they are ever going to get any better. If a child is incapable of performing a task as well as you would like, be patient. Success will come in time. You must be willing to accept less than perfection when they first start taking on new assignments.

Naturally, it is frustrating when you find patches of grass that have been missed by the mower, dirty spots on a supposedly clean kitchen floor, or grit and smudges on the just-cleaned bathroom sink. It goes without saying that in the beginning the work will probably not be done as well as you could do it. Show them, guide them, be available to lend assistance and answer questions—but remember, they are just learning. Be *patient* with their awkwardness and their delay; be willing to *tolerate* less than you would from yourself or from an older, more experienced child.

For your little ones, the results are not as important as the process. One day while refinishing the old kitchen chairs, two-year-old Levi got a piece of sandpaper and enthusiastically tried to do his part. We all praised him and commented on how cute he looked. He worked steadily for quite some time before someone finally noticed that he had the sandpaper upside down! Even though he wasn't really making any significant contribution, his accomplishments were not nearly as important as his perception of what he was doing. He *felt* important and helpful; and he was learning that when the family worked, we all worked.

"But my children are capable," you may be saying, "but still they do not perform as well as I would like." If this is the case, the problem could be a training problem. Be sure they know exactly *what* you want done, *how* to do it, and *why* it must be done a specific way. (See *Be Specific* and *Demonstrate,* pp. 22 and 29.)

If you ask your seven-year-old to clean the bathroom sink, and he doesn't do it right, whose fault is it? Sometimes we blame the child when the problem is the result of poor training. Never *assume* that your child knows how to do a task.

Too often I ask a child to do something only to discover sometime later, usually when they are half finished with the project, that they aren't doing it at all like I expected. And often I realize that I didn't spend any time explaining exactly what I wanted done and how to do it. A few moments of explanation at the outset would save us both a lot of frustration. (Remember Isaac and the bag of laundry soap.)

If you ask your child to turn the outside sprinkler off, don't *assume* she is going to roll up the hose and put the sprinkler away too. (Even if she's seen you do it that way a hundred times.) And if you tell her to put the sprinkler away, don't *assume* she will put it away where it belongs. But if you say, "Please turn the water off, roll up the hose, and put the sprinkler away where it belongs," then you can expect things to be done properly.

Expect the best they can give, but also accept the best they can give. Do your part to ensure success by providing adequate training, but at the same time, be willing to tolerate less than perfection, especially with your little ones. Tolerance, however, does not mean accepting intentional sloppiness. If you know your child is capable of more, if he did better last week, if he is angry about doing the work or in a hurry to play with friends, have him do the job again—rewashing dirty dishes or remopping the bathroom floor. You may even need to call him home from playing with friends to redo work that isn't acceptable, but it probably won't happen too often.

If *you* are consistent, they will soon learn it is easier to do it right the first time. Once they know what your expectations are, they will perform at that level. Keep your standards high. "People turn out the way you expect them to turn out. Your expectations as a [parent] are not lost on your [children]. [Children] have a way of rising to the level that you set for them. If you have faith in their ability to develop new talents and improve performance, pretty soon they'll believe they can do it too."[3]

I FIND IT ENJOYABLE

Principle—If you keep all the plums for yourself,
the only thing left for others is the pits.

Maybe you really do enjoy housework or yard work—some people do. However, by freeing yourself from some of these tasks, or at least shortening the time for their completion, you will have time for other things that you may enjoy even more. The ultimate goal, remember, is to provide opportunities for work and growth for your children, thereby teaching them responsibility while simultaneously raising their self-esteem.

Pass on your love of work to your children. Whether you love to cook, sew, garden, grow flowers, tinker with machines, or build things, involve your children. Working together provides extraordinary opportunities to glean knowledge in a hands-on way. Perhaps in the process, they will learn to love to do what you love to do.

Be careful not to delegate only the trivial, mundane tasks. Let children do those things they perceive as fun or grown up— operating the tiller, mixing bread, waxing the car, or frosting the cake. Sometimes there is a tendency to reserve a few "pet" projects for ourselves.

While cleaning up her garden one year, the mother of a six-teen-year-old son decided that he was capable of operating the tiller. Instantly, that decision gave her an extra hour of time that she would normally have spent tilling. More important, it did something signif-icant for her son. Her actions told him more powerfully than words ever could, "You're a man now. I trust you. You can do it." Hence the caution against being too lenient when assigning tasks.

Delegate something you find enjoyable for something you may discover to be even more enjoyable. It is entirely possible that there is something you enjoy doing more than cooking and cleaning! It may be something as noteworthy as pursuing a college degree or starting your own business. Or it may be as simple as having time to enjoy life's little pleasures—reading a book, going for a walk, enjoy-ing a sunset, or taking a much-needed nap.

I'M A CREATURE OF HABIT

Principle—If you always do what you've always done,
you'll always get what you've always got.

Habits can be broken. Flexibility is the first rule of delegation. This is when the first two steps of delegation become so important. (See *Decide* and *Divide*, pp. 23 and 24.) Make a list of all your every-day jobs, then ask yourself, "Could the children be doing any of these tasks?" If so, divide the jobs among family members.

One mother, upon deciding that her children could now do more, asked her son to do a job that he was not accustomed to doing. He protested indignantly, "That's not my job!"

She, in turn, responded simply, "It is now."

Scrubbing potatoes, peeling carrots, dressing a younger child, straightening a shelf, and setting the table are simple tasks requiring little time to complete, but in the few minutes you spend on those projects, you could accomplish other tasks that the children may not be able to do—going through the mail, cleaning off a counter, sorting through a stack of papers, or writing a birthday card or a thank-you note. When combined, these little projects produce big results in your overall feeling of accomplishment.

Notwithstanding the many little things children can do to be helpful, I must point out that I don't spend my days running to find a child every time there's a simple task to complete. If I spend ten minutes getting someone to do a five-minute job, my efforts are counterproductive. And sometimes when all the children are playing happily outside or are busy with quiet projects around the house, I'm perfectly content to let them be. Sometimes the peace and quiet is worth the extra effort of doing it myself. *But* if there's fighting or teasing or chasing through the house, you can be sure that I will quickly find something for them to do.

Take time to sharpen the saw. There I am—running around crazy with a dozen things to do, all of which need my immediate attention. And there are my children—reading, riding bikes, playing games, chasing through the house. So caught up in my own dilemma, I sometimes forget to take advantage of the great potential source of help that literally surrounds me. It may take a few minutes to stop, analyze the situation, and marshal the resources of my children; but in the end, it will save a lot of time and stress.

Force yourself to think of new ways to do things. This may mean changing your schedule or your mind-set. Just because you have cleaned the bathrooms at 10:00 a.m. on Monday for years, doesn't mean they couldn't get just as clean on Thursday at 3:00 p.m. We tend to function better on a schedule, so it's easy to get into a routine or to develop a certain mind-set about how things *should* be done around the house. I can tell you from personal experience that you *can* learn to do things another way that will be equally satisfactory.

When my older children were young, I liked to clean house first thing in the morning, doing the major chores while I was ambitious and had more energy. However, when I started homeschooling, I soon realized that those early morning hours were also the best time for teaching the children, capturing their minds while they were still fresh and alert and ready to learn. Consequently, housework soon took back seat to school. I learned, in spite of my preconceived bias, that it *is* possible to mop floors, vacuum, and clean the bathroom in the afternoon. I spent the morning hours doing school with the children. In return, they helped me clean house in the afternoon.

A few years later, when the older children started going to public school and their afternoons were filled with homework, I again analyzed the housecleaning situation and decided we would do the majority of the housecleaning on Saturday, allowing the children more time to focus on their studies during the week.

Although I mention these changes in routine rather casually, I can assure you they definitely took some getting used to. The house was not always as clean as I would have liked; but under the circumstances, it was the best solution. After the initial adjustment phase, however, the new schedule became the accepted routine and life went on quite satisfactorily.

Catch yourself doing things you shouldn't. As I stooped to pick up yet another toy lying carelessly on the floor, the thought came to me, *As long as you keep picking up their toys, you'll always be picking them up.* Children are happy to let you do as much as you will for them. If you always pick up their toys, put away their clothes, or clean up the bathroom after them, you will be doing it forever. Stop. Ask yourself if you have created a habit; if so, make the necessary change.

Flexibility is the first rule of delegation. Change is inevitable. Be prepared and willing to accept it.

I'M NOT ORGANIZED ENOUGH

Principle—Maximizing minutes minimizes messes.

Getting organized is a never-ending battle. Honestly, I don't know that you ever get completely organized with small children at home.

As soon as one thing gets cleaned, something else is a mess, and just because the kitchen was clean this morning doesn't mean it is clean now. I can't tell you how many times I clean off my kitchen counter every week. As soon as I do, the children come home with school papers or the mail comes, and before I know it, it's cluttered again. "Cleaning your house while your kids are still growing is like shoveling the walk before it stops snowing."[4]

I certainly don't claim to be an expert in this area. The truth is that I have a lot of ideas for getting organized, but implementing them is another story. However, there are a few things I have found to be helpful in maintaining some degree of sanity.

Go to bed with a clean house and a plan for the next day. "Psychologists claim we enjoy our evening and weekend pursuits a lot more when we leave the office with an organized desk and a plan for the next day."[5] This is true of our homes as well. This doesn't mean immaculate from floor to ceiling, but at least gather up all the toys (even if you just stack them in a corner of the room), wash the dishes, straighten the kitchen, and have children pick up the clothes and toys in their bedrooms. Doing little things the night before can make a big difference in getting off to a good start—putting dishes away, mixing orange juice, or getting bread out of the freezer. (*If* we even have any bread in the freezer.)

When we lived on the North Shore of Oahu, Hawaii, we were forty-five to sixty minutes from the major shopping centers in our area, so "going to town" was quite an ordeal. Once a month, we ran all our errands, stopping at several stores along the way. By the time we returned from our shopping trip, it was about 9:00 p.m. Tired after a long day, we unloaded the van, put away the perishables, and left the rest on the counters. I dreaded going into the kitchen the next morning. Before the day even began, I was off to a bad start. Going to bed with your house in a general sense of order will make a tremendous difference in how you feel the next day.

Keep a planner of some sort. It need not be elaborate or expensive. (I use the five-dollar one my husband gets at the university bookstore.) The only specific times I write in my planner are appointments. It would make me crazy if I wrote "10:00—clean bathroom" or "2:00—pick raspberries." For me, being that structured would be a straight path to stress and insanity.

I use my planner to keep track of the little things that so often slip through the cracks—mending a shirt, writing a thank-you card, making a phone call, cleaning a drawer. How many times have you noticed something that needs to be done and thought to yourself, *When so and so gets get home, I'm going to have him clean his dresser, straighten that drawer, or sweep the porch*? Then, a few days later, you notice the same unfinished project and realize you never asked anyone to do it. That's what your planner is for—keeping track of the little tasks that need to be completed. I also use it to plan the sequence of tasks to be completed, thus making the most efficient use of my time. And, if you have a plan for your day, it is easier to determine which tasks can be delegated.

Make lists. I keep a shopping list in my kitchen. The entire family knows it is there and how to use it. When they open the last jar or can or box of something, they are to write that item on the shopping list. The idea is that when I go shopping, I can get everything I need in one trip. (Assuming everything was written on the list in the first place.) Other lists are also helpful—mending to be done, projects to complete, odd jobs for the children. Keeping lists clears your head of a lot of clutter.

Keep clutter contained by maintaining control. "It is so much easier to keep up than catch up."[6] I have found it much easier to keep the house clean if we have periodic clean ups throughout the day. Clean up the dishes and the kitchen immediately following breakfast, lunch, and dinner. This is much easier to do when the food hasn't dried to the dishes and the countertops, and you will enjoy being in your kitchen much more if it is orderly. When my children were younger, we had a quick cleanup of toys before lunch, before Dad got home, and again at bedtime. We also tidy things up before leaving the house for any extended period of time—it makes coming home much more pleasant.

Make the most of the minutes. Take advantage of those short, unexpected time periods that occur throughout the day as discussed in the previous section. Get your children doing more. Find ways of gaining an extra ten or fifteen minutes here and there. It's amazing what can be accomplished in just a few minutes of concentrated effort.

With ten children, I consider it a miracle if I have more than fifteen uninterrupted minutes. If I waited for extensive blocks of time to pursue lengthy projects, I would never accomplish anything. I made curtains for my kitchen in twenty- to thirty-minute time segments, maybe an hour when I was lucky. We refinished our wooden chairs over a period of two months, working only thirty to forty minutes a day. And this book has primarily been written in brief, sporadic, unpredictable time snatches, with the exception of those wonderful evenings when my dear husband runs the household so I can lock myself away for a few hours of quiet time. Someone has actually calculated that if you waste fifteen minutes a day, that's two weeks of lost time a year.[7] Imagine what you could do with an extra two weeks!

Finally, don't expect to organize everything all at once. The very thought is overwhelming. Think small. Make a plan. Set a goal. Just for today you can straighten a drawer, organize a closet, or clean a room. Bit by bit, day by day, room by room success can be realized. A marathon is not run in one giant leap but in small, persistent steps one after the other. Likewise, the key to achievement in our lives is not found in great blocks of uninterrupted time but rather in short, steady, consistent efforts.

I FEEL SORRY FOR THEM

Principle—Pampering hinders productivity.

Don't feel sorry for them! You are not hurting your children at all by making them work. On the contrary, learning to work will be one of the greatest blessings of their lives. Through work, they will learn responsibility, accountability, and dependability while simultaneously boosting their self-esteem. The children you really should feel sorry for are those who don't have any responsibility. "No man needs sympathy because he has to work. Far and away the best prize life offers is the chance to work hard at work worth doing."[8]

Don't let your children lure you into the trap of self-pity. They do this ever so cunningly, with comments like, "I always do all the work," "I did it last time," "It's not my turn," "None of our friends have to work as much as we do," or "The Parkers are going camping today; why don't we ever do anything fun?" Admittedly, it can be a bit more challenging to get your children to work if the neighbor children are outside playing. But if you're sly about it, you may be able to con the neighbor children into helping too. If not, let your children know how grateful you are for their help, and keep telling yourself that you're really doing this for their own good. Someday they may even thank you.

After visiting with a mother about teaching children to work, she commented that she too believed in the importance of work. She went on to say that she had already been teaching her children many of the things we had discussed, but it was reassuring to know that she was not being a mean mother when she made her children work. As an afterthought she added, "Or at least, now I know I'm not the only mean one!"

"The greatest firmness is the greatest mercy."[9] All too often we focus on the importance of play at the exclusion of work. "They're just children," we say. And at the risk of seeming cruel or unkind, we trade momentary pleasure for our children's future happiness and success. While childhood is a once-in-a-lifetime experience, we must not shortchange them with such short-sighted reasoning. There is sufficient time in our children's lives for both work and play.

The world is a child's laboratory, filled with intrigue and wonder, ever beckoning to be explored, and children should be allowed sufficient time for a thorough investigation and scientific analysis of their surroundings. In other words, there should be plenty of time to run and play and daydream and just enjoy being a child. I firmly believe in the uniqueness and brevity of childhood, and despite my children's seemingly endless list of chores, they do not work from dawn to dusk. I assure you they have plenty of spare time.

Nevertheless, play is a privilege to be earned, not a right to be demanded. "[W]hen pleasure or recreation becomes an end in itself, we are in danger. We are in trouble. We simply cannot expect to refine the substance of character from the husks of pleasure."[10]

THEY DON'T DO IT MY WAY

Principle—There's more than one way to skin a cat.

Is your way the only way? Be willing to relinquish some control. Is it really that important that the dishes are stacked in the cupboard just so or that they've made their bed with the feet at the wrong end? Or is it more important that they are learning to put the dishes away and change their own sheets? Explain the essentials—the what, why, and how—and then leave them alone. Children really can be creative. They may find a better way to do things or they may find a way that for them makes the task more enjoyable or more tolerable. Once your children have been sufficiently trained, don't stand around looking over their shoulders, nagging and scolding.

While cleaning the fridge recently, I asked nine-year-old Marissa to take everything out of the shelves in the door. The top shelf held the butter and leftover mayonnaise, ketchup, and soy sauce samples from fast-food meals. From time to time when opening the fridge, one of these little packets would slip onto the floor and have to be retrieved and carefully placed back in its spot—tucked behind the butter to keep it from falling off the shelf. When putting the food back into the shelves, however, I noticed that Marissa had placed all the miscellaneous condiments in a little plastic sandwich bag, keeping them all neatly together to avoid future mishaps. I stood looking at the bag for a long moment wondering why I—after all these years—had never thought of such a simple solution to this annoying little problem. This day I gladly welcomed her way of doing things.

One summer I decided it was time to catch up on the children's scrapbooks. Realizing that my teenagers were now old enough to do their own, I solicited their help. Although reluctant at first, they soon caught the spirit of it. I had hoped they would spend at least an hour on the project, but they ended up spending the entire evening at the kitchen table, cutting and gluing, laughing and reminiscing. Not only did they have an enjoyable time, but I was delighted to discover that they had also done an excellent job, adding decorations and captions that I would have considered too time consuming.

At our house, my younger children iron the pillowcases. I know . . . I know. Ironing is becoming a lost art. A friend has already informed me that pillowcases don't really need to be ironed. And when I mention the word *iron* to my sister, she gives me a strange, quizzical look and asks, "What is that?" She *must* know what it is, though, because she keeps an iron as part of her antique collection. Nevertheless, at our house we still iron—and pillowcases are good practice for younger children.

The problem is that they fold the pillowcases in half lengthwise, then in fourths; I fold them in thirds lengthwise, then in fourths. As you can guess, this creates a problem when stacking them in the linen closet. In the beginning, I tried to get them to do it my way. It was after all, the way I had been doing it for years—and my mother before me. But my way was too hard for the children; and in the end, they did what worked best for them. Finally, in order to keep the stacks of pillowcases from toppling over in the closet, I decided to break with tradition; and *I* began doing it *their* way. I decided it really didn't matter, and it wasn't a battle worth fighting.

Do not misinterpret your children's revelry as detracting from the work. In reality, the merriment actually enhances the work. Think back to your most pleasant childhood work experiences. What makes them memorable? Most likely, there was some sort of fun associated with them—laughing, talking, singing, games. Do you remember much about the drudgery of raking up fall leaves, or is the memory that lingers in your mind, the fun you had playing in the leaves *after* they were raked?

I remember shelling peas by the hour as a child. The job itself was tedious and boring and the days were long and hot. We could have easily lost interest after the first bucketful, but we made it fun by laughing and joking and setting up contests to see who was the fastest or who could shell the most peas. I also remember considerable discussion over who got to tend the baby when he cried. We all adored Steven, but he was never more loved than on those long work days when he provided a welcome diversion from the task at hand. The most important thing that sifts back to me now is the good times I had with my sisters.

At the end of one summer, I asked my three younger boys to clean up the melons in the garden that hadn't ripened. If I had been doing the task, I would have taken a wheelbarrow to each melon plant, picked up the melons, and then moved on to another plant. My boys, however, seeking to find some fun in their fate, placed one boy at the edge of the garden with the wheelbarrow, another boy was positioned half way between the wheelbarrow and the melon plant, and a third boy picked the melons off the vine. He then tossed the melons to the second boy, who in turn tossed them to the boy by the wheelbarrow. My method and theirs produced the same end result. I am sure theirs was more fun.

I have also noticed my children sharing meaningful time together at the kitchen sink while washing dishes. Sometimes they talk about the school day—sharing frustrations and challenges or relating a funny incident. Sometimes they recite lengthy passages from their favorite movies, the two of them conversing back and forth as if they were the real actors. And, sometimes, my oldest daughter liked to serenade her dishwashing partners with renditions of her favorite songs—much to the chagrin of her dishwashing partner!

Still, there will be times when they get distracted with the play and forget that they should be working. Like the time I sent my three younger boys outside to shovel the driveway while I prepared dinner. Just as I was thinking how grateful and proud I was that they could work unattended, the telephone rang. It was my neighbor. She wanted to know if I knew that there were children on my roof!

Somewhere in the shoveling process they decided that *playing* in snow was more fun than *working* in it. When I quizzed them about their misplaced priority, they eagerly demonstrated their creative use of winter snow and slanted rooftops—slithering on their bellies like penguins from pitch to perch. Questioning the safety of their activity, they quickly pointed out the mound of snow built up along the edge of the roof, assuring me that their newfound sport was perfectly safe. Realistically, even if they had fallen off, it would have only been a six-foot drop into a snow-filled flower bed. But since sliding on shingles does not increase their lifespan and since the driveway was only half shoveled, that was the end of that.

Do not create drudgery. The importance of making work enjoyable was reinforced one summer while working in the garden. The first day we weeded, my daughter, who has a get-down-to-business style, suggested that everyone do their own row. That way, everyone could do their fair share and would know when they were finished. This seemed like a reasonable solution, and we each set about doing our work.

The next day, however, my oldest son was home. On this day, the children sat clumped together, sharing the work on just two rows at a time, laughing and talking as they went. Time passed more quickly, and the children hardly noticed they were working. I noticed a difference between the two days, and one of the children commented on the difference too.

We adults are too serious. We focus too much on bottom lines and end results. And sometimes we think that our way is the only way or, at least, the best way; and we try to convince our children that because we are the adults, we know best. Too much emphasis is placed on *how* the work is getting done rather than *what* is getting done, and efficiency too often takes precedence over enjoyment. In our hustle-bustle, day-timer world, we often miss out on the simple pleasures of life by failing to find the fun in what we do.

Children, on the other hand, are very clever at finding ways to turn the most mundane tasks into some sort of game. As long as the work is getting done, leave them alone. Finding fulfillment in our work does not necessarily come from doing what we enjoy but rather from learning to enjoy what we have to do. As the years roll by, the misery of the work will be remembered less and less while the companionship and merriment is remembered more and more . . . unless there was no merriment . . .

MY CHILDREN AREN'T CAPABLE

Principle—If you think they can or can't, you're right.

You might be surprised at their capacity—I was. At eighteen months, Marissa could set and help clear the table (and she insisted on helping), a two-year-old can rinse and stack dishes, a three-year-old can vacuum a small room, an eight-year-old can mow the lawn, and a fifteen-year-old can prepare an entire meal from scratch.

When my three oldest children were young, we lived in a house that had carpet in the kitchen. It was almost impossible to keep up with the crumbs on the floor. On really busy days, I would ask my three-year-old to vacuum. Then I could at least tolerate being in the room.

Out of necessity, we found out just how capable our children were during a very busy, very stressful summer. I was in the last trimester of pregnancy with our eighth child and my husband was acting as the general contractor of our new home, which consumed every spare minute. Consequently, this left the children in charge of the outside chores—feeding the chickens, gathering the eggs, feeding and milking the goats twice a day, and bottle feeding the baby goats three or four times a day. They also did all the weeding and watering in the garden and kept me informed of which vegetables were ready for harvesting. I was pleasantly surprised to see how well the children managed with very little supervision. In addition, they had their regular household chores, summer yard work, and our usual canning of fruits and vegetables. They did all of this, by the way, without getting paid for any of it—which is the topic of another section. (See *My Children Expect to Get Paid*, p. 85.)

Do not underestimate the capacity of your children—even the little ones. They like to please, and they can sense when they are performing "grown-up" work and will respond accordingly. Resist the urge to say, "Let me do it," or to shoo them away, saying, "You're too little." This merely reinforces the idea that they aren't capable and trains them to be lazy. Even when the task really is too difficult for small children, there is usually some part of it they could do. Find something—even if it means more work for you and makes the project take a little longer.

Give them a chance. There is no magical age when a child suddenly becomes old enough to help. Rather, it is a gradual process that should begin as soon as they show interest in helping, which usually happens shortly after they begin to walk. My first child followed me around the house as I did my work. When I mopped, he mopped; when I weeded, he weeded; and when I washed dishes, he stood on a chair and rinsed. If you keep telling them for the first eight to ten years of their lives that they aren't old enough or big enough or strong enough, then when they really are old enough, big enough, and strong enough, they won't want to help. Pampering produces nothing of substance.

Obviously, a young child can't do everything you do, but you will find that he loves to show off by doing as much as possible in order to prove how strong or smart or capable he is. As he grows older, he will be able to do more and more; and before you know it, he will be working right alongside the rest of the family because you never told him he couldn't.

I found out by accident that my six-year-old could change the sheets on her bed. While I was changing the sheets on my son's bed, Jadee asked if she could make her own bed. Impulsively, I thought to myself, *She's too little to make her own bed, but I'll let her try until I'm finished here.* Much to my surprise, when I finished with my son's bed, Jadee had finished hers. Unfortunately for my daughter, she had just proven she could take on another job, and that became her and her older brother's permanent task whenever the sheets were changed.

Little children love to help. They especially enjoy helping in the kitchen. They love to chop, dice, peel, grate, and stir. When they are "helping," keep in mind two rules of delegation—patience and tolerance. Allow extra time for the task to be completed and plan on things being a bit messy—sometimes a lot messy. But if you have the time and the patience, they really can be quite helpful.

One night I was cutting broccoli for dinner when my two-year-old brought a chair and insisted on "helping." He really was in the way and hindered more than he helped, but I let him rinse the pieces of broccoli and hand them to me anyway. With each succeeding broccoli stem, I sensed his self-esteem growing. Piece by piece, we grew a little closer in those few precious minutes we shared at the kitchen sink. The task may have taken a little longer, but it was well worth it.

A word of caution. Be sure your children know how to properly use the tools, equipment, and cleaning supplies that may be necessary to complete a task. They need to be aware of the dangers involved. My children learn early on how to properly use a knife, and they do very well. However, one day I was tending a neighbor boy, who used a knife to cut an apple and ended up cutting the end of his finger off.

Another time my fifteen-year-old son was whipping cream with the electric beaters. Being an unusually creative and resource-ful child, he soon discovered that the beaters could rest on the lip of the bowl and whip the cream by themselves. "Look, Mom!" he exclaimed, much pleased with himself. I nodded indifferently, then returned to my work, assuming that my old-enough-to-know-better son would grab the beaters and continue using them the way they were intended to be used. Suddenly I heard a strange, sputtering sound and spun around just in time to see the beaters lying sideways in the bowl—cream flying everywhere!

My son quickly placed himself between me and the bowl, assur-ing me that all was well. I knew otherwise. I also knew that as upset as I was, this was *not* a good time to discuss it. Muttering something about never leaving rotating beaters unattended, I turned to leave the room. As I walked away, I heard him exclaim, "OWWW . . . OW, OUCH, OOO!" Apparently, the wet beaters—still plugged into the electrical outlet—had given him a surprising zap when he tried to retrieve them from the cream. Between being shocked and scrubbing down the kitchen, I decided justice had been served.

Don't expect too much. Let your preschoolers do as much as their attention spans allow. They may work for a while, then run off to play. Some days they may surprise you by how intently they stick with a project, and the very next day they may be completely disinterested. Some days four-year-old Levi fussed and complained when asked to set the table; other days he volunteered to set it. Gradually they will be able to do more and more, working longer periods of time.

My very rambunctious, energetic little Jarom came to me several times one day asking what he could do to help. (I'm not sure what came over him.) I was very preoccupied and really didn't have anything for him to do, but I thought of something anyway—sweep the floor and pick up toys. That task complete, I suggested that he clean the sink in the children's bathroom. He hesitated momentarily and then agreed. *Surely this will satisfy his desire to work,* I thought. But his enthusiasm wasn't waning and before long, he was back again, eager for another assignment. This time I asked him to clean my bathroom sink. He hesitated a little longer and then replied in a very grown-up tone, "Two sinks in one day . . . that's kind of a lot for a seven-year-old, but I guess I will."

Teach them that when the family works, they all work. Even though the little ones may not make a significant contribution, it is important that they *attempt* to help or at least play nearby while chores are being done. Do not send them to play with a friend or leave them in the house with their toys or the television. They will learn much by watching the family work. And, by making even the smallest contribution, they will come to perceive themselves as helpers.

One morning we were all out weeding flower beds. Four-year-old Levi and eighteen-month-old Melia started out with good intentions. They pulled a few weeds and dug around in the dirt a bit. However, they soon lost interest and spent the rest of the morning wandering around the yard, chasing and playing nearby while the rest of us worked. Levi, however, was anxious to get on with the "business" of the day, which included playing with his two older brothers and was tired of waiting for them. Bored and exasperated, he declared impatiently as he strolled leisurely across the lawn, "I'm getting tired of working!"

Realize that mistakes will be made. It is important that these mistakes are used as learning experiences and stepping-stones to greater achievement. Talk about what went wrong and why. Were you partially to blame? Were the expectations unclear? Was there insufficient training? Is it possible they weren't really capable of performing the task given to them? Attack the problem without attacking the person. Try to ignore the faults unless they're crucial. *Praise in public, reprove in private.*

Find something to praise in every task, even if it's only the effort itself. One day, three-year-old Caleb came into the kitchen, took me by the hand, and led me to the bathroom. He stood there beaming proudly as he showed off the bathroom sink that he had just "cleaned." To *him* it was a symbol of success—a special surprise that he had undertaken without being asked. To *me*, it looked like a big mess and a lot of extra work. There were puddles of water on the counter and grit all over the sink. At that moment, there were a lot of things I could have said: "What are you doing?" "You're too little to clean the bathroom sink," "Don't get into that stuff unless Mommy helps you," or "Look what you've done; you've made a big mess, and now I'm going to have to clean it up." Any one of these comments would have burst his little bubble, telling him he had failed. Fortunately, I had my wits about me this day, and instead I said, "That was really nice of you to clean the bathroom sink without being asked. You're such a big boy!"

I didn't need to mention any of the truth that would be detrimental to his self-esteem nor did I need to say anything that was untrue such as "What a good job you did." He hadn't done a good job. What he had done was create extra work for me, *but* he had done it with good intentions, and the least I could do was praise his noble effort. Because of the sense of achievement gained from cleaning the sink that day, he cleaned it again a few days later—much to my dismay! But I'm a pretty fast learner. When I realized a pattern was evolving, I decided to help him learn to do it better so he could actually be helpful. I said something to him like, "That's so nice of you to clean the sink. Let me show you a few things." I then proceeded to show him how to rinse the sink, wring out the cloth, and wipe off the counter tops. Before long, he could do it very well, and I was grateful I hadn't crushed his first feeble attempts at being helpful.

Everyone has an emotional bank account; make deposits in your children's often. Praise and encouragement can go a long way in helping a child find success in a difficult project. It is amazing what children will willingly and voluntarily do when they feel their efforts are valued and appreciated. "You catch more flies with honey than you do with vinegar."

When Jadee was three, she straightened the shoes in her brothers' closet without being asked. Then one by one, she brought each family member to see her accomplishment. A few words of praise was all it took for her to do it again and again week after week.

Children are capable of much more than we often give them credit. Provide opportunities for them to prove themselves. Let them prove you wrong!

MY CHILDREN ARE TOO BUSY

*Principle—Work expands to fill the time
allotted for its completion.*

Sure they're busy, but are they busier than you? Do they make wise use of their time? Do they spend too much time texting, watching television, playing computer games, or just goofing off? Do they procrastinate? Do they dawdle? Are they overscheduled? Can some of the things they're doing be eliminated or consolidated? For your own sanity and for their future success, you can't afford *not* to give them jobs around the house.

Many children really are very busy. They are involved in sports, church, music, debate, drama, and jobs outside the home. But there needs to be balance. Their lives should not be so consistently over-scheduled that there is never time to mow the lawn and help clean the house.

At the foundation of family life there are basic household chores that need attention on a daily, weekly, and monthly basis. Regardless of the pressures we have as adults, we still have to do laundry and dinner. Children too need to understand that whatever else they may be involved in, it is important that their chores are performed in a timely fashion if the family is to function properly. Their busy lives are only going to get busier when they have their own home and family to care for. *Now* is the time for them to learn important skills such as time management, goal setting, and establishing priorities.

Teach them to work faster and smarter. Help them learn to multitask and plan the sequence of their tasks to make the most efficient use of their time. Cleaning the bathroom, for example, can take ten minutes or two hours. Obviously, the two-hour job will be (or should be) a much better job, but we do not always have two hours to spend cleaning the bathroom. And while you would certainly not want everyone doing a ten-minute job every time the bathroom was cleaned, a ten-minute job is better than no cleaning at all. Not every task needs to be done one hundred percent every time. It is fair—and promotes a lot of goodwill—to allow busy teens to cut corners occasionally.

Be flexible. There will be times when children are extremely busy. Make allowances. Do quiet deeds of service—sweeping a floor, making a bed, washing the dishes. That which goes around, comes around, and those little acts of kindness will reap large rewards in your behalf when you are especially busy. After all, that's what being a family is all about—helping each other during times of crisis. And when it comes right down to it, there are times when *you* let the weeds grow a little taller, the laundry go a little longer, or purchase pizza or takeout for dinner.

MY CHILDREN COMPLAIN

*Principle—Complaining is a child's way
of testing a parent's resolve.*

Like cows put out to pasture, children have a need to see just how far they can push the fences. Naturally, they will try to get out of as much work as possible. But once they realize *you* are serious, *they* will be more serious about doing the work.

Permanent delegation lessens conflicts and complaints. This is one reason family councils are critically important. They eliminate the need to continually argue over whose turn it is to do a job or whether it's even fair for them to do it at all. If the *who* will do *what* has already been hashed out in family council, there will be no need to continually discuss it every time it needs to be done. Children will already know they have agreed to do certain chores; furthermore, they know that everyone else knows.

Permanent delegation also helps children feel a greater degree of ownership for a task. Now it becomes *their* job instead of just a job Mom or Dad has asked them to do. Hopefully, this will motivate them to assume more responsibility and take greater pride in getting it done.

When we first got our dairy goats, my husband did all the milking. Before long, Trenton learned to milk and was asked to fill in when my husband was running late or had other commitments in the evenings. He usually performed this task under great protest and after much pleading on my part. As he became more competent at milking, we eventually decided he was old enough to do the milking every night. We explained to him that this would now be his new responsibility. The very next day he did the milking without even being asked—no complaints, no fussing, no pleading, no arguing. I was amazed at the difference permanent delegation had made.

Be polite; treat them with respect. Say please and thank you. *Ask* them to do things rather than telling them. "Would you please take out the garbage?" "Could you please help Johnny brush his teeth?" "Do you think you could set the table?" "I would really appreciate it if . . ." Now, of course, children must understand that when you *ask* them to do something it is not really a question but merely a polite way of telling them to do something. Do not let them refuse. (See *Discipline* and *My Children Refuse to Work*, pp. 32 and 73.) And be sure to notice the good things they do and take time to thank them.

Explain at the start of the day what will be expected. Children have plans too. Even if their plan is to just watch television all day, it is still a plan; and they become irritable when you keep throwing interruptions into their schedules. This frustration can be alleviated if they know at the start of the day what is expected of them.

At breakfast on Saturday mornings, we outline the necessary duties for the day, discussing any activities the children may have and deciding how everything will be accomplished. This makes it easier for the children to incorporate chores into their schedules. By knowing ahead of time what will be expected of them, there will be fewer complaints because there will be fewer surprises.

Include your children in decisions. Let them feel part of the process—make it a team effort. When there are several things that need to be done, I tell the children which chores are available and let them choose one or two they would like to do.

Give them a choice between two jobs. If you step out the back door and ask your child to set the table, what is the typical response? "No!" Naturally, he would rather play basketball, ride his bike, or continue swinging. However, if you say, "Would you rather set the table or make a salad?" you eliminate the playing option and shift their thinking from a choice between work and play to a choice between work and work.

He may even ask a few questions before making his decision: "Do we need knives, spoons, *and* forks? Do I have to grate carrots for the salad?" His little brain is assessing which job is faster, easier, or more enjoyable. Then, without even realizing that there is still the third option of doing what is he already doing, he will agree to one of *your* choices. It's a simple mind game, but it works extremely well. Occasionally, he may try to outsmart you by choosing "neither." When this happens, I simply say, "That's not an option. Choose A or B." (By the way, more than one mother has told me that this technique works well with husbands too!)

One day nine-year-old Isaac and I were cleaning up the kitchen after lunch. When we finished washing the dishes, he thought the work was done and was ready to play. However, I still needed help. I knew that asking him to sweep the floor was sure to cause an outburst. Instead, I asked, "Would you like to sweep the floor or wash the table?" By allowing him the opportunity to choose, the work didn't seem as burdensome. In fact, he washed the table without any complaint, not even realizing that he had just been part of a conspiracy!

Make it a game. There are dozens of ways to make work more fun. Have races, set the timer to see how fast they can go, pretend to be a garbage truck picking up toys, or close your eyes and see how much they can get done before you open your eyes.

I have four boys rather close in age, which means that there has been a lot of John Wayne/Roy Rogers action at our house. When they are in the middle of an intense chase, that is *not* the time to ask them to get something from the basement for me. However, if I tell them that I am sending them on a dangerous mission to a far off dungeon where they need to rescue three cans of tuna, suddenly my project becomes part of the play, and they dash off in daring pursuit. I have heard many heroic tales of dangers encountered in my very own basement while retrieving cans of this and jars of that from my own fruit room shelves!

When my two youngest were in diapers, my husband came up with a diaper-changing game. In true male style, he found a way to involve all the older children in this messy project. Whenever a diaper needed changing, my husband and children played the paper, rock, scissors game to see who *got* to change the diaper. There was always a lot of anxious excitement as they played to find a winner. It became the game the children dreaded, but this unpleasant task was made less miserable by turning it into a game.

Rotating jobs can add variety and make chores less mundane. Variety is the spice of life, and this is never more true than when it comes to chores. At our house, we change housecleaning chores on a weekly basis, but we rotate dishwashing chores daily.

Growing up, there were four girls in my family. Two of us did all the dishes for a week, then we traded. We did the housecleaning chores for several months, switching when we felt a need to change.

What chores are rotated and how often will vary from family

to family. These changes will depend on your children's personalities, their ages, and their capacities. Ask *them* what they want to do. While some children enjoy change and variety, others may not. Some children, especially young children, need consistency in order to feel secure and learn to do a job well. Be sensitive to their individual needs.

When six-year-old Isaac first entered the weekly cleaning schedule with the older children, he was overwhelmed by some of the tasks. Some of them were too hard for him, or so he thought, and the idea of doing something different each week was overwhelming. It was too much to take on all at once. So, rather than causing a lot of frustration for all of us, we simply let him do the same task every week while the other children continued with their weekly rotation. Because he felt competent and comfortable with his assignment, he did it without complaint. This arrangement worked so well, that we used it for two years. Eventually, after persistent lobbying from the older children, he joined the regular rotation and was very successful.

Offer to trade. Sometimes when the children complain, I offer to trade their work for whatever task I may be doing, which is almost always less appealing, and immediately the task I have asked them to do doesn't seem so bad after all. Occasionally, though, they do want to trade—mowing the lawn for fixing dinner, washing dishes for bathing the little ones. This can be a welcome change of pace for both of us. But don't offer to trade unless you are willing to do so!

Help them see the bigger picture. Sometimes when one of my daughters complains about all the work she's done that day, I put my arm around her and teasingly say, "Now you know what it's like to be a mom." Or "You think you've got it bad now, just wait until you're a mom." Obviously, our children will never fully appreciate what it means to be a parent until they are parents themselves. Still, we can help put things in perspective for them by discussing what it is like to be an adult. Perhaps then the work they are asked to do will not seem as difficult in comparison.

Point out the value of what they have accomplished. When a child finishes a difficult task, ask them how they feel inside. For example, if I pass by the bathroom just as someone is finishing the mopping, I may say, "Wow! That looks nice. How do you feel now that it has been cleaned?" Or, after a long day of canning, I may say, "Look at all those peaches. Think how good they will taste this winter." By helping them reflect on their sense of achievement and savoring for a moment the feeling of a job well done, they will learn to appreciate the work they do.

MY CHILDREN REFUSE TO WORK

Principle—A child's performance is proportionate to a parent's persistence.

If your child is in a complete state of rebellion, the problem may be more extensive than the scope of this book. However, I do have a few suggestions that may be helpful for your typical rejection.

Let them cool down. When a child says he isn't going to do something and storms off angrily, that is *not* the time to demand that he obey. Leave him alone for a while, giving him time to cool off. After a few minutes of pouting, the child usually realizes how ridiculous he just acted and that you haven't asked him to do anything unreasonable. Furthermore, he will hopefully recognize that what you have asked him to do is not nearly as difficult as what *you* are doing. Interestingly enough, by allowing the child some time and space to reflect upon his actions, he will often end up doing the work without any further argument.

The other day I asked my daughter who was standing idly in the kitchen to get some green beans from the basement. Even though she wasn't doing a thing, she protested indignantly, "No! It's always me. Why don't you ever ask anyone else to do anything?" Without saying a word, I continued putting dishes away. Before long, she walked closer to the cupboard and asked apologetically, "Do you want cut or sliced?"

If, after sufficient reflective time, however, the work has not been done, talk about the problem rationally. Sometimes there are legitimate reasons the child feels resentful about doing what you have asked him to do. There may be other issues you are not aware of or things you may have forgotten. Maybe he has an important test to study for or maybe you have asked him to do something every time he passed through the kitchen while another child has kept a low profile in her room all day. He may justifiably feel that he is being treated unfairly. By talking about it civilly and sympathetically, you may be able to solve the problem without further escalation.

One day I was feeling stretched to the limit. Not only had it been an unusually busy day, but I was in charge of dinner that evening at the church for twenty girls and their mothers. By the time I got the baby down for a nap, it was mid-afternoon, and I was starting to panic. Realizing there wasn't enough time to get everything done, I asked my daughter for help in mixing up a batch of roll dough. She rebelled emphatically, "NO, I WILL NOT MAKE ROLLS!"

Hurt and surprised by her outburst, I gave her a verbal lashing. I pointed out how busy I was and how selfish and inconsiderate she was being. Certainly anything she was doing was not as pressing as being responsible for feeding forty people that evening. Normally she did not respond so vehemently, and I wondered what had prompted it.

When I talked to her about it later, I understood and even sympathized. She had been trying all day for a chance to work on a quilt she was making, but she had been hit with a constant barrage of requests to do other things. She too was feeling frustrated. She explained that if I had asked her at the beginning of the day to make rolls, she would have felt differently. She could have included it in her plans and found a way to work it in. But for me to spring it on her at the last minute was the final straw.

And, sometimes, despite their initial refusal, all they need is a jump start in order to take off with a project. I asked four of my children to muck out the chicken pen one day. They worked diligently for two hours, hauling wheelbarrow loads of manure to the garden and putting down fresh straw.

A few days later, I asked the same children to rake up the horse manure in the field, scoop it into a wheelbarrow, and dump it on the garden. One son, undoubtedly feeling picked on since they had just recently been asked to do a major, messy project, had a teenage version of a two-year-old tantrum. As we are taught to do with two-year-olds, I ignored him, and he got over it without further fuss. They all trudged out to the field and worked diligently for an hour.

At length, Melia came into the house very disgruntled and demanded, "Why do we have to dig thistles too?"

"I didn't say you had to dig thistles," I explained coolly.

"Did Dad say?"

"No."

There was an awkward pause, then a sudden look of revelation about the surprise she had just spoiled, followed by a sheepish plea. "Just pretend you never heard me say thistles, okay?" And she hurried back outside.

Apparently the son who hadn't wanted to work in the first place was insisting they also dig thistles "so they wouldn't spread seeds and cause more work for them in the spring." While digging up these obnoxious weeds, they noticed trash that had blown against the fence, so they cleaned that up too. Once my son got started, he couldn't quit; and I was grateful I hadn't given in to his initial protest.

Turn off the TV . . . and the computer . . . and the cell phone. These are distractions to even the best of workers, and you can help your children stay focused by eliminating as many distractions as possible. You will be amazed at how much better your children work and how much more they can accomplish without unnecessary diversions.

You will also be amazed at how much faster they get their work done if it needs to be done *before* they play and *before* their friends come over. Have you ever noticed that the work tends to be done more sloppily and more hurriedly if their friends are hanging around waiting to play? Work will be a greater priority if they aren't distracted by more appealing prospects.

Hold family councils. I cannot stress enough the importance of a non-threatening environment for voicing opinions and frustrations.

Truly listen and try to understand from your children's point of view. Evaluate what is working and what is not. It is possible to reach mutually agreeable compromises.

Family councils make the whole delegation process seem more formal and your children will feel more committed if they have agreed to do something in the presence of the entire family. Furthermore, children will take it upon themselves to act as work watchdogs—constantly on the lookout for siblings who are not performing their work as agreed. Peer pressure alone can be a great motivator.

You may need to use the metaphorical "cannon." If reminding your child of the family council and petitioning his cooperation is not cutting it, you may need put away the "water pistol" and use the "cannon" (see *Discipline*, p. 32). The cannon should pack enough punch that performing the work becomes more appealing, but the size of the blow will vary from child to child.

Every child has limits—beyond which resistance is no longer advantageous. Car keys and cell phones are great motivators for teens; playing Wii or other computer games works well for some children; and for others it may be as simple as watching a favorite television program, riding their bike, skateboarding, or playing with a friend. It may take several attempts, but as a parent you are best qualified for figuring out what motivates your child.

At one point, I was completely baffled about getting my son to do his work in a timely fashion. He dawdled and daydreamed and was easily distracted. Every day was the same ongoing, wearisome battle. I tried bribery; I tried scolding; I tried punishing; I tried ranting and raving; I tried begging and pleading but to no avail.

Being the oldest of the three "little" boys and approaching his teenage years, he resented being treated like a child. Every night at bedtime, he would beg to stay up a little longer with the "big kids." One night while tucking him into bed, it dawned on me that staying up later was the leverage I needed to get him working.

First thing the next day, I sat him down and explained the new plan: If he did his work well without any scolding or nagging and finished by noon, he could stay up a half hour longer than his two younger brothers. If he didn't do his work well, he would go to bed at the same time. The change was miraculous!

Discipline is a balancing act. The tricky part is finding a solution that is firm enough to teach a lesson, yet not so harsh as to create resentment. If you are too lenient or inconsistent with consequences, there will be no motivation to do the work. Most children will naturally take the path of least resistance. However, being too strict creates feelings of bitterness and anger toward parents and work. The answer lies somewhere in the middle.

It's a delicate balance, and you may not always get it just right. That's part of the trial and error. If you tend to be too soft, work on becoming stricter. If you have been too strict, be willing to acknowledge it and apologize if necessary. Children are very forgiving people; and they will forgive more readily if they know that you meant well, that you are sorry for your mistakes, and that you are trying to improve. "Positional power gives the [parent] the right to give orders; however, it's the personal power earned by being considerate to and respectful of others that gives him or her the right to expect those orders to be carried out effectively."[11]

SOME CHILDREN WORK BETTER THAN OTHERS

Principle—Individuality is acceptable, indolence is not.

Anyone with more than one child knows how unique each child is. This individuality shows up in their work as well. Some children are more self-motivated, some are more conscientious, some work better with others, some work better alone, and some need more instruction or praise.

My two daughters, for instance, have very different personalities. If I were to ask them to organize their barrettes, ponytails, and hair pieces, the one daughter would do it with precision, separating them into tidy little containers by color, size, and style. The other daughter, however, needs more coaching. Knowing this about her, I can give more detail at the outset, being very specific about how to sort and which containers to use, thus eliminating a lot of frustration in the end because of unmet expectations.

I noticed a sharp contrast in work ethic between two of my sons recently. My first son spent most of Saturday working steadily and meticulously on a bug collection for his biology class. When that was complete, he moved on to other homework, studying late into the evening. About nine that same night, my second son, who had spent most of the day in numerous frivolous pursuits, stretched out on the couch, hands tucked behind his head and said with his characteristic quirky grin, "Ahhh . . . this is the time of day when I assess the homework situation." I thought I was going to blow a gasket!

No matter how hard you try, some personality traits will never change. The challenge of parenthood is matching the child with the chore. By understanding your children's uniqueness, you can better tailor the work to fit their individual needs.

Workers and slackers—every family has them. I know who the slackers are in my family, but each time we do a project, I give them a chance to overcome their slothful tendencies. From time to time, they surprise me. But, usually, I end up giving a warning.

After a child has spent twenty minutes pulling the same weed, for example, I will encourage faster performance by threatening to assign a specific section of the garden or flower beds to weed. Children who are not picking their share of raspberries will be assigned a measurable quantity of raspberries to pick. For children who squabble over the work in their shared bedrooms, you can divide their duties or assign separate days for cleaning.

By dividing the work, a slothful child cannot rely on others to do his work, and you can inspect what he has done to determine if it is satisfactory. Working together as a family is an excellent way to build unity, but care must be taken to ensure that everyone shares the work. Sometimes the better workers carry the bulk of the work while the less-willing workers coast.

Avoid the "oldest child" or "best worker" syndrome. There is a natural tendency to delegate to the oldest child or the best worker (which are very often the same person) simply because they are more capable, more dependable, or more experienced. This practice strengthens their work ethic and self-esteem while encouraging laziness among the less ambitious. It can also cause the oldest child to feel overwhelmed and picked on, thus developing feelings of resentment toward parents and siblings. It requires conscious, deliberate effort to ensure that each child learns to work.

Being the oldest child in my family, I understand the importance of equal distribution of chores. Once when my mother was preparing to leave, she gave me a list of tasks to perform while she was gone. A bit perturbed that she hadn't told any of my three sisters to do a thing, I can remember grumbling, "What are the other girls going to be doing?"

When you leave the house, make a written list outlining chores for each child to complete. This gives them individual assignments for which they can be held individually accountable. It also eliminates excuses such as, "I didn't know," or "I forgot." And it helps prevent the older children from being too bossy and the little ones from being picked on.

Let each child specialize in certain tasks. Just as the oldest child shouldn't do all the work, they also shouldn't get all the privileges. Let each child be the first to learn or do something new. By allowing a younger child to be the first to learn to iron, sew, make bread, or wash the car, you create in them a sense of expertise. At our house, twelve-year-old Camille puts the two-year-old to bed at night, Isaac is my carrot peeler, and Caleb is our expert mashed potato maker. This does not mean, however, that they perform these tasks exclusively. Even though children may develop expertise, cross-training is essential in a family as well as in business.

No boy or girl jobs. This cross-training applies to gender as well. My only brother was barely eight when I married, so my sisters and I never knew there was such a thing as "boy and girl" jobs. In addition to our inside chores, we learned to mow the lawn, feed chickens, weed the garden, dig potatoes, and shovel manure. And the same is true of my own daughters.

A mother who had only sons taught them domestic housekeeping so well that when their wives had babies, they assumed all the cooking and cleaning while their wives recuperated. Each wife has personally thanked this mother for her foresight in raising such wonderful homemakers. Likewise, my sons are learning to cook, sew, iron, mop floors, wash dishes, and change diapers. My goal is for each child to be as competent as possible in running a household before leaving home.

Don't become discouraged, though, when this swapping of roles doesn't go as well as expected. Eighteen-year-old Camille had changed the oil in the family car more than once, but this was her first time changing it in her own vehicle. On a cold January day, she bundled up in warm clothes and coveralls and asked her dad to guide her onto the car ramps. After careful maneuvering, she was ready to go to work. At this point, my husband inquired about the oil and oil filter.

She stared at him blankly, then asked incredulously, "Don't we have some in the garage?"

"I don't have an oil filter that will fit *your* car," he replied.

Disheartened, she backed her car down off ramps, unbundled, and trudged into the house. Back too soon, we all wondered aloud how the oil changing had gone. She walked through the room without a reply.

The next week she purchased oil and a filter, and a few days later she once again bundled herself up in warm clothes and coveralls and drove her car up on the ramps—thirty minutes before she was supposed to go babysitting. (Thirty minutes would be sufficient time for an expert mechanic. Our daughter was no expert.)

She tried in vain to loosen the bolt on the drain plug and finally solicited help from one of her older brothers. With all the delay, there were now only ten minutes before she needed to leave. At last the reality that had been so clear to the rest of us when she started this undertaking, suddenly became clear to her—there would not be time to change the oil today. Once again, she backed her car off the ramps, unbundled, and trudged dejectedly into the house.

They say things come in threes. A week later she bundled up in warm clothes and coveralls and drove her car up on the ramps. (With all that practice, she was getting pretty good at it.)

Today she would be successful. She had no place to go and no unforeseen hindrances. The drain plug came off easily and all was going as planned. Pleased with her progress, she leaned closer to check that the oil was draining properly, leaning right into the draining oil! Luckily, she was wearing a hat.

I'M STARTING TOO LATE IN THEIR LIVES

Principle—You can *teach an old dog new tricks.*

It is never too late. In fact, the older your children are, the greater urgency you should feel to teach them all they need to know before they leave home. Old habits are hard to break but not impossible. Obviously, it is easier to get children working if it has been a way of life since they were young. However, with effort, older children can be "persuaded" to work. Don't give up. Start small and gradually add to their responsibilities. With consistent effort, positive results can be achieved. (See *Discipline* and *My Teenagers are Intolerable,* pp. 32 and 82.)

Older children can better understand your needs, time pressures, and commitments. Talk about how it feels to be a parent and how crazy you feel at times. Help them understand why you need their help. And help them understand that learning to work will bless their lives too.

Don't let them leave home without the benefit of your tutelage in the basics of housekeeping. You can give your children the edge on life by taking advantage of their remaining years at home to pass on some of the tips and tricks you have learned about cooking, cleaning, laundry, home repairs, and yard work. Being on their own will be challenging enough without starting out at a disadvantage.

MY TEENAGERS ARE INTOLERABLE

Principle—"There's nothing wrong with teenagers that reasoning with them won't aggravate."[12]

We had heard all the horror stories and had received multiple warnings, "Just wait until they're teenagers!" And so it was with anxious dread that we approached our oldest son's thirteenth birthday. But nothing happened. He seemed to glide through the teenage years unaware of the perplexing role he was supposed to be playing. My husband and I looked at each other and said, "What is the big deal?" Then . . . we had more teenagers. And we have now joined with thousands of baffled and befuddled parents for the most tumultuous roller coaster ride of our lives!

Teenagers—what a peculiar group. They're old enough to think they know it all and too young to know they don't. I believe most teenagers don't mean to be obnoxious. Most of them know how to be civil and decent. In fact, most of them do very well at church and school, with the neighbors, and with their peers. In reality, it's a power struggle.

Don't back down. Getting your adolescent to work may be more difficult, but it is crucial that you persist *and* insist that they do their part. Don't let their independence and their stubbornness fool you. They really do want you to make them mind. They want to know there are limits of what you will and will not tolerate. The same rules of discipline still apply, although the consequences may need to be a little more firm. You may need to use the "cannon" more frequently. (See *Discipline* and *My Children Refuse to Work,* pp. 32 and 73.)

My sister's teenage son lives to play soccer, but his grades were suffering. Determined that his success in soccer would not come at the sacrifice of his success in school, my sister marched onto the field one day during practice. In spite of the incredibly embarrassing scene she created and despite his desperate pleadings for mercy, she dragged him home to study. Amazingly, his grades improved immediately.

Communication is the key. One of the best ways to show that you value your teen's opinion is to seek their advice. As teens become increasingly independent, they want to have a more active role in what goes on around the house. They want to feel appreciated and respected. That accomplished, they will be much more willing to do their part.

Communication is not only important with regard to work but in all aspects of their lives. When the children were younger, my husband and I had been accustomed to making the decisions about family outings. The general pattern had been for us to discuss it between ourselves, then announce our "exciting" plans to the children. This method backfired on us several times. At last it began to sink in that if wanted our older children to be happy participants, we needed to counsel *with* them *before* making plans.

Respect their time. With a new job for my husband, a new baby, and a new-to-us home on three and a half acres, our first summer in Hooper was extremely busy. Consequently, I relied on my children heavily. It seemed as though I was always asking someone to do something—changing diapers, fixing meals, cleaning up toys, folding laundry. My husband also called from work regularly, asking the children to do various projects in the yard. One day it dawned on me—especially after the roll incident with my daughter—that our children had little time to call their own. At any given moment, they may be called upon to do something. The roll incident was the impetus for our weekly planning sessions and for more detailed daily discussions about what we expected them to do while allowing time for personal projects.

Weekly planning sessions. On Sunday evening, we gather as a family to discuss our plans for the week. We learn about our children's plans and commitments, and they learn about ours. It may take some prodding to get your older children to enumerate their plans, and there will naturally be unexpected things that come up during the week, but it is important to identify as many activities as possible in order to alleviate potential conflicts. It is all written down on a calendar that is posted in the kitchen. This way the children can make plans for incorporating chores and other projects into their schedules while allowing time for themselves.

Play together. All work and no play creates ill-tempered teens. Interact with them in ways other than work. Start traditions—homemade ice-cream, Sunday night popcorn, family read alouds, sports, movie night, fishing and hunting, camping and hiking, playing games around the kitchen table. Go shopping with them. Help them decorate their room. Spend leisure time with them. Laugh with them. Enjoy being with them.

Love them and be their friend. Get to know them as real people. There is nothing a teenager needs more than a true friend. They will do almost anything for a friend. Why not use that to your advantage? As astonishing as it may seem, this can be a great time for parents. I am enjoying my teenagers. At last I have children old enough to carry on intelligent conversations and old enough to be incredibly helpful. If they know you and like you, they will be more willing to work with you and for you.

Although it doesn't always show on the surface, a teenager yearns to be loved, needed, and accepted. The saying, "When they deserve love the least, they need it the most," is especially applicable at this stage of life. Love can overcome so many things.

Learn to let go. Young adults have lives too—often very busy lives. They have plans and goals separate from yours. Recognize their need for greater independence. Be willing to let them make more decisions for themselves. Also be willing to let them suffer the consequences of those decisions.

One Sunday I decided to keep most of the children home from church since they were quite sick and had terribly croupy coughs. When my fifteen-year-old son learned about the plan, he was quite put out. He wanted to know why he couldn't stay home too. He whined and moaned about how unfair it was. When this got him nowhere, he finally agreed to go to *part* of church, walking home two and a half miles if necessary. This threat did not get the reaction he had hoped for, so then he tried the I'm-feeling-sick-too ploy. This didn't work either, and at last I told him to go to his room and think about what he wanted to do.

It wasn't long before he came into the kitchen, completely dressed for church. With an air of confidence, he announced smugly, "*I* have decided that I *want* to go to church. I want to go to *all* of it too, and I'm *glad* to do it."

What he was really saying was that this was *his* decision and he didn't want to be coerced into doing anything he didn't want to do. I was prepared to let him stay home if it came to that. Thankfully it didn't. By allowing him the opportunity to choose, he came around to the right decision on his own and was much happier about it. If you treat your teenagers with respect, viewing them as the adults they are trying to turn into, the results can be miraculous.

MY CHILDREN EXPECT TO GET PAID

Principle—Money cannot buy a strong work ethic.

My philosophy is that children should not get paid for doing basic chores around the house. After all, you don't get paid for the work you do. Weeding, laundry, making beds, cleaning house, washing dishes, preparing meals, shoveling walks, and mowing the lawn are necessary aspects of family life, and children should learn early on that it takes a lot to keep a household running. They need to learn to work out of a sense of obligation toward the family, not for the reward. Our family motto is, "He who works, eats!" Although it is said in jest, the message is clear.

Even still, when asked to do something, my children will occasionally question, "What will you give me?" or "What do I get?" To this inquiry, I respond simply, "You get a good feeling in your heart." My husband's typical response is a little more practical, "We're going to feed you dinner tonight." Another mother says, "I'll start paying you for the things you do when you pay me for the things I do."

Teach your children to cherish the satisfaction that comes from serving others. Great joy comes from doing what needs to be done, with no thought of personal gain. A life lived for self is a lonely one indeed.

One Saturday morning I was vacuuming for a child who would be gone all day. Halfway into the project, nine-year-old Marissa generously offered to finish since her chores were already done. With a very busy to-do list, I gladly consented, most grateful for this unexpected, compassionate reprieve.

As fourteen-year-old Abram walked past our yard one day, he thought to himself, *The garden looks nice and the yard looks nice, but that patch of weeds in the irrigation drain ditch looks horrible.* Two days later, while watering the garden, he decided to pull the entire patch of four-foot high weeds. This was not a simple task and took considerable time and effort, but it made a huge improvement in the curb appeal of our yard. I was grateful for his selfless service.

Nevertheless, it doesn't hurt to reward your children from time to time—a trip to the library, making cookies, a sleepover with a friend, or watching their favorite movie. On hot summer days when we are weeding the garden, I will sometimes say, "Let's hurry and get this done, then we'll have a popsicle." Or if we have an especially busy Saturday, we occasionally try to make it more tolerable by promising to make homemade ice cream at the end of the day. Rewards can help take the drudgery out of work and can motivate children to work faster and more cheerfully, but they should be offered infrequently to be most effective. They must be the exception, not the rule, in order that children do not come to rely on them. If your children regularly ask for or expect a reward, they are probably getting them too frequently.

After a recent snow storm, Marissa helped Camille shovel the driveway. Although Marissa helped voluntarily, upon completion of the task she tried to coerce her older sister into some sort of tangible compensation. Camille offered no reward. While Marissa was initially disappointed, when she recounted the event to me several days later, she beamed proudly, "You know what I got, Mom? I got a good feeling in my heart!" Gratefully, my nine-year-old was learning that sometimes the best reward is no reward at all.

It is a false notion that bribery is the only way to get children to work. Children want to feel productive. They want to make a positive contribution and know that their efforts are appreciated. Little children, especially, want to be part of everything you are doing. By capitalizing on their innate curiosity and willingness to help when they are young, they will grow up being naturally helpful.

> It is a myth that children don't want to work. Most children love to work and often offer to help. . . .[W]e can reject the popular idea that children must be prodded, enticed, or supplied with any external motivation to participate in family chores.
>
> When we speak of motivating others, we accept a nearly universal belief among social scientists that all action begins with the self. Supposedly, a person's need . . . or their desires . . . prompt them to act in their own interest. In theory, then, the way to alter another person's behavior is to appeal to that self-interest by dangling rewards in front of them. . . .
>
> When we train children to work by paying them, whether with money or privileges, we reinforce self-interest. While this approach may have positive results in the short term, it often disintegrates into manipulative attempts by both parent and child to outmaneuver one another.[13]

The decision to give your children an allowance is a personal one. But they will be better off in the long run if you resist the temptation to tie allowances to daily chores. If they need extra money, find something for them to do above and beyond normal household tasks. One mother posts a list of jobs available for cash on the refrigerator door—cleaning the fridge or oven, washing baseboards, and vacuuming out heat vents. When a child needs a little spending money, they can choose one of the extra jobs *after* doing their regular chores.

Better yet, let someone else pay them. Even young children can find profitable work outside the home. They could get a paper route or do odd jobs for neighbors—dog walking, babysitting, lawn mowing, snow shoveling, window washing, or leaf raking. There are dozens of entrepreneurial ideas for the creative and the ambitious. I recently received a cute email that sums it up well: "I figured out at a young age the easiest way to get money from rich people—it's called a job."[14]

When I was young, my father cut up our surplus banana squash, weighed it, priced it, and put it in our little red wagon. We children went door-to-door, selling it to the neighbors. We were thrilled with the prospect of earning a little spending money.

Before moving to Hawaii, my four oldest children shared three paper routes. They bought their own bicycles and roller blades. Because they used their own hard-earned money, their purchases meant more and they took better care of them. And since moving back, my younger children have accumulated size-able savings accounts by hoeing acres and acres of onions for the local farmers in the fields surrounding our home. It is menial labor to be sure, but they have been grateful for the privilege of working for pay.

One year we ended up with thirty bushels of apples from our five apple trees. We sorted them into small paper bags, and our four youngest boys, ages five to ten, set out down the road, selling them to the neighbors. Since the blocks in our neighborhood are one-half mile long, making it a two-mile walk around one block, this was quite a commitment. Because of the distance involved, I expected them to go to a few close neighbors on our street before giving up. They surprised me, however, with their perseverance. They spent all afternoon walking the "neighborhood," coming home just long enough to drop off the five-year-old who was getting tired, get a drink of water, and pick up more apples. By the end of the day, they had spent more than five hours peddling apples and walked nearly five miles. It's amazing what children will do when motivated to make money.

Instead of using monetary rewards as motivators, try positive reinforcement. Sometimes the best payment of all is a loving pat on the back, a few words of praise, or a genuine thank you—verbal or written. We are never too young or too old to appreciate a compliment.

I enjoy being told "thank you" for those daily tasks mothers are "supposed" to do. Even though I wash and iron my husband's clothes every week, it certainly makes the effort seem more worth-while when he notices what has been done and takes the time to thank me. Thank your children occasionally for the chores they are "supposed" to do. Notice when they do a little extra or when they do a job especially well.

Ideally, a little recognition is all the payment children should need. However, sometimes it takes a little more to get them started initially. From time to time I had trouble getting the little ones to make their beds, brush their teeth, get dressed, and comb their hair in the morning. I could spend the morning nagging and scolding or I could inflict some sort of punishment, but I found that a little positive motivation worked much better. Setting the timer for fifteen minutes, I told them that if they were ready when the timer rang, they got to pick a treat. At first they wanted the treat immediately, but after a few days they forgot to ask for it until twenty to thirty minutes later, then an hour, and then maybe half a day. Before long, they no longer needed the candy at all. All they really needed was a little help in forming a habit. This same kind of motivation works well with homework, practicing the piano, or any chore that seems especially difficult or demanding.

Brag about your children. Brag to others about the good things your children do *when they're around.* It is fun to watch their faces light up as they beam with pride while trying to look embarrassed. Make it a point to mention to Grandma or the neighbor that your eight-year-old can now mop floors, your five-year-old cleaned the bathroom sink today, or your three-year-old is learning to make his own bed. When we have company for dinner, I mention the part each child has played in the preparation of the meal. A little public recognition goes a long way in bolstering self-esteem and making children want to perform even better the next time. As the saying goes, "A child may not always remember what you say, but he will always remember how you made him feel."

Be careful when praising, thanking, or bragging. Don't overdo it. If done too frequently or excessively, it can be harmful. Avoid using excess flattery or being too gushy. These techniques are similar to working for pay, and children learn to work for external recognition rather than their own internal sense of accomplishment. An occasional, sincere, heartfelt compliment is much better. "The real key to praise is that it's got to be spontaneous. . . . [It] has to be natural.... If you really love people, and care about them, you won't build a phony kind of relationship."[15]

Other incentives. When I notice that a child has done an exceptional job or has been especially helpful, I tape a little note to their bedroom door in recognition of their effort. These are made of colorful paper and displayed for all to see. They may earn one of several awards that are represented by corresponding pictures:

- Busy Bee (bee)—doing something that is especially hard or time consuming
- Helping Hand (hand)—helping more than usual, especially without being asked
- X-tra Miler (large X with "mile" in the center)—exceeding expectations
- Happy Helper (smiley face)—cheerful attitude, saying "sure" or "I would be glad to"

On the award, I write the child's name and what they have done. Not only is this a fun way of saying thank you, but it also gives them a little public recognition for those extra efforts that often go unnoticed. And, hopefully, this subtle motivation will inspire the other children to do a little more.

I realized these awards were having some impact when I overheard my five-year-old explaining to one of his friends about the "X-tra Miler" award that was taped to his bedroom door. I am sure the little friend had no idea what my son was talking about, but I was impressed with how much this minor recognition meant to my child.

Chore charts. Many parents like to use chore charts and stickers or other visual incentives to inspire industry. I have seen some pretty creative charts, and I think there is some merit in this approach. Colorful charts are certainly appealing to young children, and they can be helpful initially in getting them used to the idea of doing chores and having daily tasks.

The drawback to chore charts is that they are one more thing for *you* to do, and they tend to have short-term effects. If the motivation to work comes from the sticker or the chart, then as the newness and excitement wears off, you will find yourself with the added burden of continually making new charts and coming up with increasingly clever incentives to keep your children working.

Our chore "charts" consist of little sticky notes on the corkboard in the kitchen listing the order of the rotations for Saturday chores, dishwashing, and lawn mowing. There are no stickers or boxes to check. They simply serve as reminders when the children forget which assignment needs to be done next. And when the rotation changes, the "charts" are easy to replace.

Getting your child to work is not unlike potty training. Initially, with potty training, we bribe the child with treats every time he uses the bathroom, but as a habit is established, the treats gradually become less and less while the expectation remains the same. So it is with work. The long-term goal is for the child to do what needs to be done simply because it needs to be done. It is absurd to think that you would give your sixteen-year-old a treat every time he used the bathroom. And, yet, we often treat our teenagers like two-year-olds when it comes to work. The motivation and the reward for work should come from within. That is where all true motivation comes from eventually.

Notes

1. Taylor, *Delegate*, 28–33, 79–86, contains further information on delegation.
2. Richard Rogers, http://www.lyricsondemand.com/soundtracks/s/the-soundofmusiclyrics/somethinggoodlyrics.
3. Arthur L. Williams, Jr., *All You Can Do is All You Can Do, but All You Can Do is Enough* (Nashville, TN: Oliver-Nelson Books, 1988), 146.
4. Phyllis Diller, *Phyllis Diller's Housekeeping Hints*, 1966, http://www.quotegarden.com/
5. Taylor, *Delegate*, 48.
6. Leo D. Bardsley

7. Taylor, *Delegate*, 54.
8. Jacob A. Riis quoting Theodore Roosevelt, "XVII Roosevelt as a Speaker and Writer," http://www.bartleby.com/206/17.html.
9. Henry W. Longfellow, "Longfellow quotes," http://brainyquote.com /quotes/h/henrywadsw151348.html
10. Gordon B. Hinckley, *Standing for Something* (NY: Three Rivers Press, 2000), 95.
11. Taylor, *Delegate,* 15.
12. Patricia H. Sprinkle, *Children Who Do Too Little* (Grand Rapids, MI: Zondervan Publishing House, 1996), 115.
13. Kathleen Slaugh Bahr, "The Sacred Nature of Everyday Work, Part 3," *Meridian,* 4, http://www.ldsworld.com/ldsworld/print/1,2143,workfamily work+library,00.html.
14. http://www.WashingtonIsBroke.com.
15. Arthur L. Williams, Jr., *All You Can Do is All You Can Do, But All You Can Do is Enough* (Nashville, TN: Oliver-Nelson Books), 149.

4

REWARDS
OF DELEGATION

Only those who do not know how to work do not love it.
—*J. H. Patterson*

At this point, I hope it is obvious that there are wonderful rewards for delegating. By way of summary and as a last ditch effort to convince you, if you are not already convinced, I will explain the benefits here. I have saved the rewards for last because I guarantee there will be days when you think raising children who know how to work is all about self-torture. Hopefully, these rewards will be fresh on your mind when you have those thoughts.

- Saves your sanity
- Creates more free time
- Enhances children's self-esteem
- Keeps children busy
- Promotes greater family unity
- Teaches children to value work
- Prepares children for the real world

SAVES YOUR SANITY

Whether you work full time or part time or are a full-time home-maker, whether you are married or single, and whether you have two children or a houseful, I think we would all agree that there is too much to do and too little time in which to do it. All too often we try to be "superdad" or "supermom," but reality dictates that we simply cannot and should not do it all. Children create the majority of our work, so it is only reasonable that they should do their part to help.

Do not play the martyr. Parenthood is stressful enough without taking on more than necessary. For the sake of your physical, mental, and emotional well-being, you *must* delegate. In fact, your sanity depends upon it!

Sometimes it is next to impossible to get things done without our children's help. For example, when our family had church at 8:00 a.m., there was no way we could make it on time without delegating to the older children. Each Sunday morning while eating breakfast, various tasks were delegated—one child prepared the diaper bag; each of the older children helped a younger child get dressed, comb their hair, and brush their teeth; and someone else did the dishes . . . then I calmly strolled to the bathroom to do my hair!

My children rescue me from an embarrassing moment. It was two days before Christmas, and I had a mother/daughter dinner that evening at the church. Since I was in charge of making all the lasagna for the meal, I got started early in the morning.

At noon, my daughter informed me that she absolutely *had* to have something from town (an hour away) *before* Christmas; and the next day being Christmas Eve, the store would not be open. Since the lasagna was already made, I figured we could run to town and still be back in time to get ready for the dinner.

Of course, the trip took longer than expected; and on the way home, I broke into a cold sweat, realizing that we would not be home in time to bake the lasagna. This was one meeting for which I could not be late! Stopping at a pay phone (I know—it's the twenty-first century, and they do make cell phones), I called home to ask my son if he could get the lasagna baking, which involved using the neighbor's oven. I also asked him to make some salad dressing for that evening.

I then drove on, feeling confident that things were now under control. But, alas, as I continued to drive, I remembered more details that had not been taken care of. Again, I started to panic and pulled over once more to call home, asking the children to do several more things. We arrived home just in time to change clothes, throw everything into the van, and take off again. Thanks to my children having everything ready, I was spared what could have been a terribly embarrassing moment.

On another long shopping trip, I called home to tell the children I was running late and to give them a few instructions about dinner. Since I knew I would be home just in time to put them to bed, I also asked if they could bathe the little boys. I was surprised and touched to hear my son softly say, "It's already been done, Mom."

These are the paydays of delegation. Obviously, payday doesn't happen every day. Just like the business world, there is an awful lot of stress and effort and plain hard work between paychecks. Likewise, payment from your children is sometimes few and far between, but when payday finally comes, you will know it has been worth it.

CREATES MORE FREE TIME

By delegating many of your routine tasks, you will have more time to work on other projects, help children with homework, manage the household, develop skills or talents, or pursue personal interests. If I can get one or more of the children to prepare dinner, I may have an extra half hour or more for exercising, sewing, gardening, or writing this book.

From our library window where I am typing, I can see several children in the backyard. The younger ones are picking up apples and branches that have fallen off the trees so the lawn can be mowed, another child is mowing the lawn, and still another is sweeping the patio. Saturday chores have already been done, and my husband is planning to make a Dutch oven dinner so I won't have to cook. Which means, of course, that several of the children will be in the kitchen helping him. . . .

I never cease to be amazed at what can be accomplished when the family works together. Housework, yard work, cleaning the garage, organizing the basement, canning, or any other project goes more quickly when everyone helps. Then, instead of *you* spending the day working while the children play, *everyone* can have some free time. Many hands really do make light work.

This book could have never been written without the help of my entire family. My husband has generously volunteered to tend children, cook meals, clean house, run errands, and change diapers so I could have time for writing. He and the children even spent Saturday afternoons making salsa and applesauce while I typed at the computer. Likewise, each of the children has gone the extra mile in helping with laundry, babysitting, gardening, and preparing meals. It has definitely been a group effort.

Parenthood is synonymous with sacrifice. Being a parent often means giving up some of our own personal goals, dreams, and ambitions—or, at least, putting them on hold for a while. But it doesn't mean giving up everything. Reward yourself with some "me" time occasionally. You cannot give from an empty cup. Doing something that is personally rewarding or fulfilling is not a selfish thing. It doesn't hurt the children at all to cook dinner while you exercise or to tend the baby while you nap. (As grumpy as I get when I'm sleep deprived, the nap is as much for the children as it is for me.)

Don't feel guilty. Taking time for you is actually a benefit to your children. Your children learn valuable lessons on work and service. You, in turn, give them the gift of a happier, more patient parent.

ENHANCES CHILDREN'S SELF-ESTEEM

One woman told how her older brother always spoke of helping their father build the family home. The woman was either not yet born or too young to remember the event and took him at his word. Years later, while reading her father's journal, the woman discovered that her brother was only four years old when the home was built! In reality he probably hindered more than he helped, but in his young-boy mind, he had actually been one of the builders. Somehow he was made to feel that his efforts were so valued that even as a grown man, he believed that he had built the house.

This experience reminds me of a Wheaties commercial on television years ago when I was a child. I don't remember all the details, but my closest recollection is of a father and son sailing on the ocean. The sun is just peeking over the horizon, and, naturally, they are eating Wheaties for breakfast. As the father turns the steering of the vessel over to his teenage son who, with a look of surprise and smug assurance, takes control, the voice in the background declares, "Wheaties . . . when a boy finally knows he's a man."

Children really do want to please, and they crave attention. One of the most meaningful ways to satisfy this need is to give them responsibility. Although they may fuss and complain and try to get out of work, their self-esteem will grow as they begin to feel they are making a significant contribution to the family.

Years ago, I watched in frustration as two-year-old Melia struggled to fasten her snaps. I thought it was a hopeless cause, but she insisted on doing it herself. When she was at last successful, she looked at me and exclaimed triumphantly, "Did it, Mom!"

While your ten- or twelve-year-old may not be quite as enthusiastic about her accomplishments, the feelings inside are just as real. The next time she does a particularly difficult task or does something especially well, notice the gleam in her eye and the look of pride on her face. She even seems to act a little older and stand a little taller as if to say, "It was hard, but I did it!"

Most children, even very small children, like to feel productive and important. At age five, my very energetic, carefree little boy suddenly became interested in helping in the kitchen. Each night as dinner was being prepared, he bounded into the kitchen to ask what he could do to help, and each night I gave him the same answer, "You can set the table." With a family as large as ours, this was a very helpful thing to do. Apparently, he did not place the same value on this task. After several nights of cheerfully setting the table, he came into the kitchen and once again asked what he could do to help. Before I could respond, he quickly added in a pouty, pleading tone, "And don't say set the table. I want to do something *important*." My son taught me a profound and powerful lesson that night.

The tasks we assign our children tell them our perception of themselves. We can do much to raise their self-esteem by giving them assignments that imply trust and approval. Provide opportunities for them to do things at the limit of their capacity. (Your fifteen-year-old can do much more than clean his room and make his bed.) Where there is no challenge, there is no growth.

KEEPS CHILDREN BUSY

Too many children spend too much time texting, watching television, playing computer games, sleeping in, and hanging out. Statements such as "There's nothing to do," "I'm bored," or "I can't wait for school to start," are reflective of their excess leisure time. Too much free time is a phenomenon unknown to children of earlier generations.

While children really do want to be industrious, most do not naturally look for productive ways to spend their time. The tendency is to choose the path of least resistance. Therefore, it may take some effort and encouragement on your part to motivate them, but the rewards will be worth it. There are so many worthwhile things they could be doing—sewing, cooking, baking, drawing, reading, painting, growing a garden, learning a trade, practicing a musical instrument, or starting a home business. Be creative. The possibilities are limited only by your own imagination.

Excess leisure and the resulting boredom is fast becoming a national epidemic. It manifests itself in society's escalating dilemma with gangs, violence, and vandalism. "The greater part of human misery is caused by indolence."[1] Idle minds are the devil's workshop. On a smaller scale, boredom in the home leads to fighting and teasing and a general feeling of unrest. Many of society's problems could be dramatically reduced if children were kept busy with productive, meaningful activities.

PROMOTES GREATER FAMILY UNITY

My four boys, ages four to ten, were doing outside chores one cold winter day. Since the outside taps were frozen, they were excitedly running back and forth to the kitchen sink, filling jugs with hot water for the animals. After several trips to the sink, I heard six-year-old Abram remark enthusiastically, "We're a team!"

Teamwork is a term generally associated with sports and athletic events, but it has application to families as well. By working as a team, victory is achieved on the baseball field, the basketball court, and the hockey rink. Likewise, success and unity in family life is realized when individual members work together toward common goals.

By working together, children learn important social skills while simultaneously developing bonds of friendship as reflected in the following testimonials of college students:

> I never realized why my older brother and I were such good friends. When we were in our early teens, we helped my dad build our house, install the sprinklers, landscape the yard, and do all sorts of odds-and-ends jobs. I remember many times when we would have to cooperate to accomplish many of our work goals. . . . Now that we are older, there is a bond that we share because we worked side by side in our developing years. I would not trade them for anything. . . .
>
> When I was in the fourth grade, my mom started a bakery business selling breads and cinnamon rolls to bring in some extra money. . . . As children, it was our job to wash the containers everyday. . . . We dreaded [it] but we did it anyway. I remember laughing so hard on some days, and I remember being so mad at my brother on other days that I knew I could never forgive him (until two minutes later when he would do something that would be so funny and make me laugh). . . . I've always felt especially close to my

brother, and I have believed for a long time that it is because we had to work and spend so much time together while growing up.[2]

One study concludes that children who work with and for family members learn to be less self-centered and more focused on the needs of the family a whole:

> Canadian scholars . . . compared children who did "self-care tasks" such as cleaning up their own rooms or doing their own laundry, with children who participated in "family-care tasks" such as setting the table or cleaning up a space that is shared with others. They found that it is the work one does "for others" that leads to the development of concern for others, while "work that focuses on what is one's own," does not. . . . In one international study, African children who did "predominantly family-care tasks [such as] fetching wood or water, looking after siblings, running errands for parents" showed a high degree of helpfulness while "children in the Northeast United States, whose primary task in the household was to clean their own room, were the least helpful of all the children in the six cultures that were studied.[3]

"Doing nothing for others is the undoing of ourselves."[4] In a very practical way, work teaches children to become less concerned about "me" and more concerned about "we." By giving of themselves to benefit another, they become less selfish and less demanding. Work literally becomes a labor of love.

It was fun to see my children's excitement over our garden the first year we moved back to the mainland. Since we didn't plant a garden the three years we lived in Hawaii, my younger boys didn't remember what it was like to grow our own food. The whole garden experience—from tilling the ground in early spring to planting and watering the little seeds and watching them sprout to harvest time—was a thrilling adventure for them.

They kept me informed all summer on the progress of the garden—the ripening of the tomatoes and each new melon and pumpkin on the vine. There was great excitement over our first ears of corn, our first zucchini, and, of course, the long-awaited, much-anticipated event of picking our first watermelon—not a day too early nor a day too late. Walking through the garden, there was a sense of camaraderie that was indescribable. It was not a fleeting, momentary pleasure but rather an enduring sense of achievement from days and weeks of laboring together.

When we built a new home a few years ago, it was a family project—putting down shingles; laying a wood floor; setting tile; sanding and staining; and sweeping, sweeping, sweeping. The children threatened to mutiny if they had to sweep one more time! But when we finished, it was *our* house. Similarly, the house we now own has required some fix-up. Through painting and plumbing, roofing and remodeling, sanding and sawing, family unity has increased.

"Teamwork divides the task and doubles the success." Your family life will be greatly enhanced as you work as a team. Work is always more enjoyable if Mom and Dad are there too. Sing songs, listen to music, tell jokes, laugh . . . enjoy being together. Your attitude toward work will rub off on your children, and these family work/play times will become cherished memories that will last a lifetime.

TEACHES CHILDREN TO VALUE WORK

A century ago, farming was the predominant occupation and the survival of the family depended upon the cooperation of every member. Children worked out of necessity. Work came naturally to them, and they did not feel picked on or abused.

While farm life naturally lends itself to the creation of work, it is not essential. The more broad and varied a child's work experience, the better. Perhaps you know a plumber, a painter, an electrician, a cabinet maker, a carpenter, a mechanic, a seamstress, or a hairdresser who would be willing to teach your child the tricks of his or her trade.

I have relatives who are dairy farmers in upstate New York. Several years ago, we sent two of our sons to spend the summer learning what it is like to be a real farmer. Because of their extraordinary experience, we recently sent two more sons. Clearly, we did not send them because there was a shortage of work at our place. In fact, their leaving created quite a lack of available laborers, and I nicknamed my two youngest daughters Cinderella One and Cinderella Two since they were home during the day trying to help me keep up with the weeding and watering.

Obviously, not every child has the opportunity to travel halfway across the country for a spectacular work experience, but that is not essential in raising children who know how to work. Everyday experiences in ordinary circumstances can teach a child much about real life. Living in a crowded subdivision or a high-rise apartment building requires greater effort on the part of parents to create work for their children, but it can still be done. Look carefully at your surroundings. You may be surprised at how much your children can learn in whatever situation you may find yourself.

Even if you're renting, there are things you can do to teach your children to work. Think of it as your place. Fix it up. Keep it clean. Care for the yard. Grow a garden if possible.

We rented for many years before purchasing our first home. In several of the places we lived, we were able to have a small garden. We always considered it a blessing to be able to work for some of our food and to supplement the grocery budget with fresh, homegrown vegetables. We also kept the lawn mowed, planted flowers, hung pictures, and made curtains. We took pride in our surroundings even though we didn't own them. In the process, we gained a measure of self-respect while providing valuable work opportunities for our children.

If you don't have a yard, there are many things to learn inside the home. Children can learn cooking, cleaning, mending, home repairs, remodeling, painting, and budgeting. They can learn to run the washing machine, iron a shirt, clean an oven, defrost a freezer, and unclog a drain. Someday they will be on their own, and suddenly they will be expected to do all these things themselves. They will be better prepared to handle emergencies and the day-to-day stresses of life if much of their daily routine is already second nature. The more tasks children master, the easier adulthood will be.

An excellent place to start is with children's own bedrooms. If children get into the habit of making their beds, picking up their toys, and putting their clothes away on a daily basis, they will not find it too difficult to keep their rooms reasonably clean. They can learn much about tidiness and organization by caring for their personal belongings. And the effects of cleaning their own rooms will naturally spill over to other parts of the house, making it easier to one day care for their own homes.

An added bonus to children cleaning house is that they are more apt to keep it clean. They will also insist that other family members keep it clean. Who is the first one to get upset when someone dirties the freshly-mopped kitchen floor? The one who cleaned it, of course. When a child has just invested a considerable amount of time and energy cleaning part of the house, they feel a greater degree of ownership over that area. And they will be the first to announce to the family that nobody better get it dirty!

One winter, my daughter, who had not been around to help with much of the canning, brought up a jar of peaches from the basement. Isaac, who had been my biggest helper that year, snatched the jar out of her hands and protested accusingly, "You can't eat those. You didn't help can them."

While eating dinner not long ago, Levi spilled on his pants. He mentioned that he would need to put them in the hamper to be washed. There was a brief pause, and then he added pensively, "Of course, that means that I will have to put them in the washing machine, hang them on the line, take them off the line, fold them, and bring them in the house."

When we reroofed the house a few years ago, it was Melia and Marissa's job to wash the dishes after every meal, allowing the rest of us more time on the roof. One day while stopping for lunch, Melia asked if she could make one of her favorite lunch menus—fried tortillas. Obtaining approval, she got the frying pan out and set it on the burner. Then she stood for a long moment, looking back and forth from her tortilla to the frying pan. Slowly she put the frying pan back without saying a word, but I knew exactly what she was thinking: *If I use that pan, I will have to wash it.*

Isaac, Levi, and Melia had learned that canned fruit, clean clothes, and clean dishes don't magically appear in cupboards and closets. Everything comes at a cost. What a blessing to learn this important lesson at such young ages. Teach your children "that the privilege to work is a gift, that power to work is a blessing, and that love of work is success."[5] "The major work of the world is not done by geniuses. It is done by ordinary people . . . who have learned to work in an extraordinary manner."[6]

PREPARES CHILDREN FOR THE REAL WORLD

"It is better to build boys than to repair men."[7] In sharp contrast to childhood, adulthood is all about work. The more children learn to work during childhood, the easier life will be for them as adults. Someday your children will grow up and out of your home and will have to face the real world. They will be better prepared for that day if they have learned the value of hard work, commitment, sacrifice, and the law of the harvest.

The philosophy "Give a man a fish, you feed him for a day; teach him how to fish and you feed him for a lifetime" applies equally to children and work. Clean your children's rooms and they are clean for a day (if you're lucky); teach them to clean their own rooms and they can be clean every day.

> We teach by habit, we teach by precept, and we teach by example. Aristotle says that habituation at an early age makes more than a little difference; it can make almost all the difference. So if you want kids to learn what work is, you should have them work. If you want them to learn what responsibility means, you should hold them responsible. If you want them to learn what perseverance is, you should encourage them to persevere. And you should start as early as possible.[8]

By giving our children adult responsibilities, we won't end up with adults who still act like children. "Children who are taught to work and to enjoy the fruits of that labor have a great advantage as they grow toward maturity. The process of stretching our minds and utilizing the skills of our hands lifts us from the stagnation of mediocrity."[9] Our job as parents is to raise competent, capable, contributing members of society. This process begins today. It occurs bit by bit as we provide opportunities for learning and growth for our children. We do our children no favors by pampering and catering to them.

Notes

1. G. C. Lichtenberg, "Lazy Quotes," http://www.quoteseverlasting .com/topic.php?c=Lazy.

2. Bahr, "The Sacred Nature of Everyday Work," *Meridian*, at http://www .ldsworld.com/ldsworld/print/1,2143,everydaywork+library,00.html.

3. Kathleen Slaugh Bahr, *World Congress of Families II*, Geneva, Nov. 14–17, 1999, 6, at http://www.worldcongress.org/gen99/speakers/gen99/bahr .htm.

4. Horace Mann, "Horace Man Quotes," http://www.goodreads.com/ quotes/show/16334

5. David O. McKay, quoted by David E. Sorenson, "Work Is a Blessing as well as a Spiritual Necessity," *Church News*, March 12, 2005, 10.

6. Gordon B. Hinckley, quoted by Sorenson, "Work Is a Blessing," 10.

7. Richard L. Evans, *Richard Evans' Quote Book* (Salt Lake City, UT: Publishers Press, 9th Printing, 1980), 62.

8. William J. Bennett, "Teaching the Virtures," Feb. 2003, 2. Reprinted by permission from *Imprimis*, the national speech digest of Hillsdale College, www.hillsdale.edu.

9. Gordon B. Hinckley, *Standing for Something* (NY: Three Rivers Press, 2000), 94.

CONCLUSION

The sleep of a laboring man is sweet.
Ecclesiastes 5:12

Hopefully, you feel empowered to combat the stumbling blocks you encounter in the daily battle of getting children to do their work. The implementation of delegation will be unique to each family in their varying circumstances. Some families are large; some are small. Some have young children, some have teenagers, and some have a combination of both. The needs of the mother and the capacity of her children also vary widely from family to family. And as the family grows, so will the capacity and responsibilities of the children.

What works with one child may not work with another. What works in the summer may not work during the school year. What worked in our home twenty years ago when our two little children began working no longer works with a houseful of children. And what works for us now will no longer work when more children leave home. While the underlying rules and principles remain fixed, there is the never-ending, ever-changing, constantly-evolving process of applying those principles in our individual families.

Delegation has boosted my children's self-esteem by giving them a sense of self-worth and belonging while simultaneously teaching them important life skills that will assist them in their ascent to adulthood. It has not been easy, but then, nothing truly worthwhile usually is. Raising children who know how to work involves a great deal of energy, and at times you will wonder if it is worth the effort. I can promise you that it is, but you must personally be convinced of that in order to put forth the necessary effort on a daily basis. I hope I have provided some convincing evidence.

Through delegation, we have experienced the effects of synergy, which means that the whole is greater than the sum of the individual members. In other words, we can accomplish twice as much in half the time. "Teamwork is the ability to work together toward a common vision. The ability to direct individual accomplishments toward organizational objectives. It is the fuel that allows common people to attain uncommon results."[1]

Many times my children have literally saved the day when something unexpected has come up or when I just had more than I could handle. Even more frequent are their simple, spontaneous acts of service—sometimes performed anonymously. I can honestly say that I could not do all that I do without the help of my entire family. Delegation has made it possible for me to do homeschool, keep up with the housework, and write this book, while raising ten children and somehow managing to maintain marginal sanity.

In today's fast-paced, frenzied world, we seem to be continually searching for those elusive ingredients necessary for strengthening family ties. Society tells us they are found in high-adventure, action-packed, expensive thrills, but you may be surprised to learn that much of what you are seeking can be found within the walls of your very own home. Too often we hurry through the chores in order to get on with our family fun and, ironically, miss out on priceless opportunities to bolster family unity.

Working together can develop a love and closeness that can be achieved in no other way. Through our labors, we build character, strengthen friendships, and create enduring memories. In our efforts to fortify family relationships, we must not overlook the remarkable binding power of quietly—or not so quietly—working side-by-side performing the simple, ordinary, daily tasks of life.

Note
1. Andrew Carnegie, "HeartQuotes: Quotes of the Heart," http://www. heartquotes.net/teamwork-quotes.html.

Appendix

When I'm not working, I get tired of myself.
—Herbert Hoover

SUMMARY OF STUMBLING BLOCKS AND PRINCIPLES

I can do it faster myself.
The best investment you can give your child is your time.

If you want it done right, do it yourself.
You get what you expect.

I find it enjoyable.
If you keep all the plums for yourself, the only thing left for others is the pits.

I'm a creature of habit.
If you always do what you've always done, you'll always get what you've always got.

I'm not organized enough.
Maximizing minutes minimizes messes.

I feel sorry for them.
Pampering hinders productivity.

They don't do it my way.
There's more than one way to skin a cat.

I'm starting too late in their lives.
You can *teach an old dog new tricks.*

My children aren't capable—
If you think they can or can't, you're right.

My children are too busy.
Work expands to fill the time allotted for its completion.

My children complain.
Complaining is a child's way of testing a parent's resolve.

Some children work better than others.
Individuality is acceptable; indolence is not.

My children refuse to work.
A child's performance is proportionate to a parent's persistence.

My teenagers are intolerable.
"There's nothing wrong with teenagers that reasoning with them won't aggravate." –Patricia H. Sprinkle

My children expect to get paid.
Money cannot buy a strong work ethic.

AGE-BASED CHORES

The following list serves only as a guide for chores children are capable of performing with little or no supervision. The ability to perform specific tasks will vary from child to child and from family to family.

18 Months–2 Years

set/clear table
pick up toys
put clothes in drawer
assist parents in *everything!*

3 Years

rinse dishes
load dishwasher
entertain baby
straighten shoes in closet
dress and undress themselves

4–5 Years

empty garbage
make bed
match socks
fold clothes
bring in groceries
dust
sweep
simple vacuuming

6–7 Years

clean bathroom sink
scrub toilets
dress younger children
chop food—handle a knife
grate cheese
rake leaves
feed bottle to baby
iron pillowcases
load washer and dryer
feed and water inside animals
sweep patio
change sheets
help can fruits and vegetables

8–9 Years

feed and water outside animals
wash dishes
mow lawn
shovel snow
weed garden and flower beds
tend siblings for short periods
prepare simple meals
mop floors
clean bathtub
vacuum
water outside plants
change diapers
wash walls
straighten clothes drawers

10—11 Years

hang clothes on clothesline
follow recipes
bathe younger children
wash windows
sew
sort laundry

12 Years

simple mending
iron clothes
babysitting
prepare complete meals
follow a recipe

Teenagers

operate equipment—
tiller
weed eater
chain saw
power tools
make bread
bake from scratch
home repairs
defrost freezer
clean refrigerator
clean oven
edge lawn
change oil in vehicles
clean clogged drains

INDEX

· · · · · · · · · · · · · ·

self-esteem, 21, 24, 50 56, 64,
66, 79, 89, 93, 96–98,
107
serve, xvii
service, xvii, 3, 68, 86, 96,
108
shelling peas, 6, 59
shower massage, 22,
slackers, 78
snow, shoveling, 6, 60–61, 87,
114
soccer, 1, 82
specific, 9, 17, 22, 25, 30, 49,
78, 113
speed, 20, 48
spontaneous delegation,
14–15 89, 108
synergy, 168

T

Taylor, Harold L., 13
team, 70, 99, 101
teenagers, 24, 28, 37, 46, 58,
81–82, 84–85, 91, 107,
112

thistles, 75
time out, 34
tolerant, 17, 20
tools, 64, 115
tortillas, 103
training, xix, 3, 11, 13, 23,
29–30, 33, 47–50, 66, 79
Trenton, 5, 15–16, 19, 69

W

washing
dishes, xvii, 1, 6, 15, 60, 72,
85
onion, 32
what, why, how, 29, 32, 58
Wheaties, 97
whipping cream, 64
wooden chairs, 7, 49, 56
work watchdogs, 76

X

X-tra Miler, 90

About the Author

Debbie Bowen is a full-time homemaker and mother of ten children, six boys and four girls. Her experience and expertise for writing this book have been gained from the day-to-day, real life struggles of raising her own children. She has given numerous workshops on the topic of teaching children to work.

In addition to writing, she enjoys sewing, gardening, trying new recipes, and making flower arrangements. One of the things she most looks forward to is her weekly date with her husband, giving her a chance to unwind and giving the children yet another opportunity to practice the principles outlined in this book.

Debbie's husband works as an administrator in higher education; as a result of his employment, they spent three years living in Hawaii. It was a wonderful cultural experience for the entire family. However, they have since moved to the little farming community of Hooper, Utah, where their children keep busy tending their 3½ acre hobby farm. They describe this change of residence as moving from one paradise to another!